Giver of Life

Giver of Life

THE HOLY SPIRIT IN ORTHODOX TRADITION

Fr. John W. Oliver

a PARACLETE GUIDE

PARACLETE PRESS
BREWSTER, MASSACHUSETTS

Giver of Life: The Holy Spirit in Orthodox Tradition

2011   First Printing

Copyright © 2011 by John W. Oliver

ISBN: 978-1-55725-675-1

        Library of Congress Cataloging-in-Publication Data
Oliver, John W., 1966–
    Giver of life : the Holy Spirit in Orthodox
    tradition / John W. Oliver.
        p. cm. -- (A Paraclete guide)
    Includes bibliographical references.
    ISBN 978-1-55725-675-1
 1. Holy Spirit. 2. Orthodox Eastern Church--Doctrines. I. Title.
    BT121.3.O45 2011
    231'.3--dc22

                              2010047571

10 9 8 7 6 5 4 3 2 1

Published by Paraclete Press
Brewster, Massachusetts
www.paracletepress.com
Printed in the United States of America

*T*o my wife, Lara, and our children—

through whom the Giver gives me Life

Contents

Preface

MAN IS LOST IN THE WOODS. He's been wandering there for many years, doing enough to survive but perpetually uncertain how exactly to find his way out. With each wrong turn, he learns a little more about both the forest and his lostness. Signs of life are everywhere. Even though he is lost, his internal compass grows gradually sharper over time, so he never panics. He just keeps moving.

One day, while walking down a path, he meets a group of people who are also lost, but they've only been lost for a few hours. The frightened group pleads with the man—please, can you tell us how to find our way out of this forest? No, the man replies, but I can tell you how not to get more lost.

That story is one of my favorite descriptions of the priesthood. My priesthood, at least. While I am an Orthodox priest, I stumble through the woods in my own way and cannot offer anything of lasting value about much, and especially not about so lofty and sacred a topic as the Holy Spirit in Orthodox tradition, a topic that requires such precise reflection that a single wrong word could lead to the thicket of confusion or over the ledge of heresy. So, in this book I try to stay to the paths worn smooth by the reflections of the saints through the ages, those men and women who have found their way—or, more precisely, allowed themselves to be led—out of the woods.

The rest of us who feel varying degrees of lostness can join ourselves with the patient but pleading soul as described in a prayer poem called "An Akathist Hymn to the All-Holy and Life-Creating Spirit":

> The life-creating Spirit, Who descended like a dove upon Christ in the Jordan, rested also upon me in the font of baptism. But the influence of His goodness hath weakened because of the darkness of my falls into sin. Wherefore, as a traveler lost in the forest at night doth wait for the light, so do I await Thy rays, O Good One, lest I perish utterly.

In *Giver of Life: The Holy Spirit in Orthodox Tradition*, the reflections of the saints—the early saints of Holy Scripture; the later saints of holy history—are evident especially in the liberal use of quotations and stories from them, but also, I hope, in how they inform my own contributions to the text. The frame around which the whole reflection is built is an ancient prayer to the Holy Spirit (a prayer the reader is encouraged to embed into his or her own prayer life). Breaking the prayer into phrases, we reflect on the truths and treasures each phrase may yield. The only additional prayer the author can make is that, in the end, all that remains of the book in the hearts and minds of readers is only what the Holy Spirit Himself has placed there.

We need the Holy Spirit to understand the Holy Spirit. As we begin, the most fitting plea for His guidance is, not surprisingly, supplied by a saint—Symeon the New Theologian (949–1022), whose own reflections on his personal and firsthand experience of the Holy Spirit have inspired seekers of the forest's edge for a thousand years:

Come, true light. Come, eternal life. Come, hidden mystery. Come, nameless treasure. Come, ineffable reality. Come, inconceivable person. Come, endless bliss. Come, non-setting sun. Come, infallible expectation of all those who must be saved. Come, O Powerful One, who always creates and recreates and transforms by Your will alone. Come, O invisible and totally intangible and impalpable. Come, You who always remain motionless and at each moment move completely and come to us, asleep in hades, O You above the heavens. Come, O beloved Name and repeated everywhere, but of whom it is absolutely forbidden for us to express the existence or to know the Nature. Come, eternal joy. Come, non-tarnishing crown. Come, purple of the great king our God. Come, crystalline cincture, studded with precious stones. Come, inaccessible sandal. Come, royal purple. Come, truly sovereign right hand. Come, You whom my miserable soul has desired and desires. Come, You the Lonely, to the lonely, since You see I am lonely. Come, You who have separated me from everything and made me solitary in this world. Come, You who have become Yourself desire in me, who have made

me desire You, You, the absolutely inaccessible one. Come,
my breath and my life. Come, consolation of my poor soul.
Come, my joy, my glory, my endless delight.[1]

Introduction

*T*HE STORY OF PENTECOST in the second chapter of the New Testament book of Acts is full of imagery that captures us from childhood—sounds from heaven, a rushing mighty wind, tongues of fire and flames over heads. Languages burst forth and lives are forever changed. So dramatically odd was the experience that the apostle Peter began his homily that day with an assurance to the onlookers that, no, those of us receiving this outpouring of the Holy Spirit are not drunk.

Jesus, risen from the dead, had ascended from earth to heaven ten days earlier. His disciples, still winded with wonder, were now gathered to tend to crucial details: stay in Jerusalem, as Christ had commanded before His ascension; find a replacement for Judas, who had killed himself after betraying Christ; and pray about what comes next. And what came next has been called the birthday of the Church.

A mighty sound filled the dwelling where the disciples were staying, as if poured into that small space from the vault of heaven. The Old Testament prophet Joel said this would happen. He prophesied that someday God would pour out His Spirit and give to the world a new power that would create wonders in the heavens and on earth (Joel 3:1–3). Then tongues as if made with

fire appeared above each of the disciples. This part of the supernatural event was predicted by the New Testament prophet
John the Baptist. Christ will come, he announced while preaching in the desert, and will baptize with the Holy Spirit and with
fire (Luke 3:16).

Filled with divine inspiration, the disciples miraculously
began to speak about the wonderful works of God in languages
not their own. This caught the attention of pilgrims who were
a long way from home, from towns and tribes far to the north
and south and east and west of the Roman Empire. Many had
come to Jerusalem as Jews, but left as Jewish *Christians*. Those
"wonderful works of God" (Acts 2:11), the apostle Peter
explained convincingly, reached their highest point in the death
and resurrection of Jesus of Nazareth.

The descent of the Holy Spirit on the disciples that day
more than energized the Jerusalem assembly; it released a
transformative power into the world that has been changing
lives ever since. "The Lord Jesus Christ sowed a most precious
seed in the field of this world," wrote the saintly bishop
Nikolai Velimirovich, "but the power of the Holy Spirit was
needed to come upon it, to give it warmth and light, and
make it grow."[2] The power then is the power now. Orthodox
Christians celebrate Pentecost as both a fixed event and a
constant reality—the Spirit who stirred the dust in first-
century Jerusalem is the same Spirit who has stirred hearts in
every age and place since.

As a liturgical celebration, the feast of Pentecost is lovely.
Winter, with its deadening blanket, yields to spring, and
Pentecost almost always falls during spring. Orthodox

Christians around the world harvest and bring new greenery of all kinds into the churches—ferns, sprigs, branches, flowers, palms, herbs, even trees.

The splash of green foliage is designed to call to mind not just life but also a special kind of life. It is the life that transcends biological existence and flows from the very Godhead Itself; it is the life that is actually a *state of being*—immortal, everlasting, changeless. Ferns and flowers fade and die, but souls filled with this "life from above" flourish forever.

This use of biological life for the celebration of spiritual life also helps to connect the New Testament event of Pentecost with its Old Testament predecessor, the "Festival of Weeks," the feast that commemorated the beginning of the grain harvest— an important season in the life of an agrarian culture like ancient Israel. "You shall observe the Feast of Weeks," the Lord spoke to Moses, "the firstfruits of wheat harvest" (Exod. 34:22).

Intimacy with the land was an inevitable result of Hebrew practical dependence on the cycles of planting and harvest but also of their solemn observance of a liturgical calendar imbued with references to the land's activity. Major feasts—Unleavened Bread, Firstfruits, Weeks—filled that practical dependence with religious significance.

But the Festival of Weeks was more than a day's observance. The celebration spread over seven consecutive weeks, beginning on the morning following the Sabbath day of Passover. Seven weeks of seven days, plus the day of Passover, equals fifty days. Later in the Old Testament, the Festival of Weeks came to be known as Pentecost, a Greek word that means "fiftieth" (Tob. 2:1; 2 Macc. 12:32).

Thinking poetically, we might say that the wheat harvest of the Old Testament Festival of Weeks became a soul harvest at the New Testament Pentecost—because of that dramatic outpouring of the Holy Spirit in Jerusalem, about three thousand converts joined the new Christian community. And the two loaves of bread required by the old festival became the two nations blessed by the new reality—God's plan of salvation was extended not just to Jews but to Gentiles too.

The Spirit Who changes lives, the Spirit Who pours forth upon all—these are among the themes we will explore in the chapters that follow. Something else we will discover in the chapters that follow, in its own way showing forth the particularly Orthodox understanding of the Holy Spirit, is *limitation*.

The mystery of the Holy Spirit in Orthodox tradition— flowing as it does from the very mystery of God in Trinity—is vast, deep, subtle, and awesome. Towering saints have devoted wells of ink to the subject, and yet we feel the trembling of even their pens as we read what they have written. The reflection of any one person is limited. For the Orthodox mind, however, this is unsurprising. And really, it's the consensus of the saints through the ages that we look to, and they tell us that *knowledge about* the Holy Spirit is gained through *experience of* the Holy Spirit—an experience deeper than words and concepts and known only to what the New Testament calls "the hidden person of the heart" (1 Pet. 3:4). "Concepts create idols," wrote Saint Gregory of Nyssa. "Only wonder grasps anything."[3]

Knowledge, if understood as information, is important. But information is limited. We may learn, for example, about the transfigured Moses on Mount Sinai without ever undergoing transfiguration ourselves; we may learn about the apostle Paul being caught up to the third heaven without ever ascending there ourselves. Any Orthodox reflection on the Holy Spirit will be an invitation to the Holy Spirit to move from the page and into the person.

When Orthodox Christians gather to celebrate Pentecost and the descent of the Holy Spirit, we frequently sing this troparion, or hymn:

> Blessed art Thou, O Christ our God, who hast revealed
> the fishermen as most wise, having sent upon them the
> Holy Spirit, and through them Thou hast fished the uni-
> verse, O Lover of mankind, glory to Thee.

We may understand "fishermen" to mean more than just men who fish, but also *simple, humble, unworldly*. The apostles upon whom the Holy Spirit descended in the upper room at Pentecost were men of simple vocation and not like those who occupied the Roman senate or the Jewish council. "The Holy Spirit hath taught wisdom to the illiterate," we sing at the Feast of Pentecost, "and hath revealed the fishermen as theologians."[4] In subsequent Church history, saints would emerge from every facet of society—from caves and palaces, from monasteries and universities. The Orthodox embrace the intellect, but we're also aware of its limitations.

So, while a book like this one about the Holy Spirit may transmit information, an interior awakening is the real goal. This is why Orthodox theological insight is embedded in our liturgical life. As we pray, so we believe; as we believe, so we pray. Prayer opens the heart to the penetrating presence of God, whose touch upon every person in every place at every time is always Trinitarian—*from* the Father, *through* the Son, *in* the Holy Spirit.

It is fitting, then, that a reflection on the Holy Spirit in Orthodox tradition would weave, like a river winding through a forest, around our most common prayer to the Holy Spirit. Indeed, this prayer is so important that Orthodox Christians rarely begin any activity of significance—indeed, rarely any morning—without it:

O heavenly King, the Comforter, the Spirit of truth, Who art everywhere present and fillest all things; Treasury of good things and Giver of life; come and abide in us, and cleanse us from every impurity, and save our souls, O Gracious Lord.[5]

This is a "fountainhead" prayer; its power flows into every other prayer. "The Spirit also helps in our weaknesses. For we do not know what we should pray for as we ought," wrote Saint Paul, "but the Spirit Himself makes intercessions for us with groaning which cannot be uttered" (Rom. 8:26). Acquire the Holy Spirit and, in a sense, *He* becomes our prayer life. Writing in the seventh century, Saint Isaac the Syrian wrote, "When the Spirit makes His abode in a person, he is no longer able to stop praying, because the Spirit never ceases to pray in him."[6]

The Holy Spirit brings us to the Son, who brings us to the Father. In this Holy Trinity is life stronger than death, love greater than hell, and unity greater than all fragmentation that relentlessly tears at our existence.

The greenery of Pentecost eventually fades. Flowers wilt, ivy dies, and the churches are purged of all browning leaves and petals and stalks. We, as creatures in time, leave the season of Pentecost and anticipate the next phase of the liturgical year. Over the months, other church beautifications will emerge—commemorating the transfiguration of Christ or the birth of Mary or the elevation of the Cross. Though the event celebrating the descent of the Holy Spirit may pass, the power of that experience never does. Instead, the Holy Spirit remains, leading to deathless life all who strive to be simple, humble, and unworldly.

Giver of Life

1
O Heavenly King

O heavenly King, the Comforter, the Spirit of truth, Who art
everywhere present and fillest all things; Treasury of good
things and Giver of life; come and abide in us, and cleanse
us from every impurity, and save our souls, O Gracious Lord.

•

LOWERS, like those with which the Orthodox adorn
our churches during Pentecost, open gradually. So
too does Holy Scripture, revealing its inner treasures
over time. Orthodoxy is an emphatically Trinitarian
faith, but the book of Genesis does not open with an explicit
and detailed explanation of "Holy Trinity" or "three Persons" or
"Father, Son, and Holy Spirit." Yet Orthodox Christians believe
that the aroma of the Trinity rises from the first page.

"Let Us make man in Our image" (Gen. 1:26). Who, exactly, is
Us? "Then the Lord God said, 'Behold, the man has become like
one of Us" (Gen. 3:22). Like Whom? "Come, let Us go down
there and confuse their language" (Gen. 11:7). Who is coming
down? These references to God are uttered by God Himself. Is
He referring, perhaps, to Himself and the angels? But why would
humanity be made in the image of both God and the angels?
Or is He referring to some plurality within Himself? But if, as

Moses wrote, "Hear, O Israel, the Lord our God is one Lord" (Deut. 6:4), how can there be plurality in *one*?

So pages are turned and petals are opened: while early Genesis suggests some kind of plurality, later Genesis hints toward *three*. The Orthodox perceive God's appearance to Abraham in the form of three mysterious visitors as rich with Trinitarian significance. A famous icon often used in churches during the season of Pentecost—by the Russian iconographer Andrei Rublev and called *The Hospitality of Abraham*—shows three angelic figures seated at table, two looking toward one, and is often adorned with boughs that represent the ancient oak of Mamre beneath which the encounter occurred (Gen. 18).

When Orthodox Christians reach the end of the Old Testament and turn around to survey the landscape covered, we see perhaps the most powerful foreshadowing of the Holy Trinity: the presence, everywhere, of "God" who gives His "Word" and shares His "Spirit."[7] Yahweh is in the midst of His people not as a concept or an idea but as Word that is also an *act* and as Spirit that is also a *presence*.

Entering the New Testament, the three come into sharper relief. "When He had been baptized, Jesus came up immediately from the water; and behold, the heavens were opened to Him, and He saw the Spirit of God descending like a dove and alighting upon Him. And suddenly a voice came from heaven, saying, 'This is My beloved Son, in whom I am well pleased'" (Matt. 3:16–17). At the baptism of Christ, the three have now been identified—God, a Son, and a Spirit.

Later, Jesus commands the disciples to "go therefore and make disciples of all the nations, baptizing them in the name of the Father and of the Son and of the Holy Spirit" (Matt. 28:19). "Name" here is singular—a vital detail. In this call to evangelize known as the great commission, Father, Son, and Holy Spirit are identified individually yet are united in some way.

More pages, more petals. In the last book of the four Gospels— the Gospel according to the apostle John, the last in order and the last written—Jesus reveals greater detail and distinction about the Father and the Son and the Holy Spirit. "And I will pray the Father, and He will give you another Helper, that He may abide with you forever—the Spirit of truth" (John 14:16–17). The New Testament Greek word for Helper is *parakletos*, or Paraclete, also translated as Comforter and found in the prayer to the Holy Spirit serving as our guide.

"These three are one." One *what*? And *how* are they one? Are the three actually distinct from each other, or are "Father," "Son," and "Holy Spirit" just labels describing different ways God interacts with His world? The New Testament identifies "Father" and "Son" and "Holy Spirit" but does not formulate an explicit doctrine about them or their relationships with each other. For that, we look to the faithful Church Fathers of the turbulent centuries following the New Testament period.

Exploring Church history expecting to find nothing but sweetness and light is a bit like exploring a hospital expecting to find nothing but well and healthy people. The content of Christian faith is important, and people struggle over important things. Often, the modern mind casually accepts much of what the ancient mind struggled to clarify. We might thumb through our pocket New Testaments, for example, without appreciating (or even realizing) how many years were spent and how much sweat was spilled over the complex matter of the New Testament's formation.

The doctrine of the Holy Trinity—sprouting in the Old Testament, blooming in the New—was the subject of vigorous discussion in the early centuries of the Church. No one was disputing the *titles* of "Father" and "Son" and "Holy Spirit," since the Scriptures frequently mention each. Instead, the questions to which answers would emerge only after great struggle were these: Who, exactly, is the Son, who is the Holy Spirit, and what relationship do they have to each other and to the Father? And these questions really mattered because, like the source of a river, their resolution would influence later Christian belief and behavior.

Heresies rose; debates raged. While struggling to grasp essential truths, men passed words with passion and urgency. The first ecumenical council, convened in AD 325 in the city of Nicaea (in what is now Turkey), was summoned, in part, to deal with a controversy surrounding the divinity of Jesus Christ. A teaching about Christ had emerged, promoted by a renegade priest named Arius, that "there was a time when He was not." This "formula," because it was rightly interpreted to be an attack on the equality of the Son with the Father, was rejected at the first ecumenical council. Church Fathers at that council declared that Christ is "light of light, true God of true God, begotten, not made, *of one essence* with the Father."

If words were passed at the first council with passion, so, perhaps, were blows. According to legend, in a fierce act for which he was immediately imprisoned, bishop Nicholas—the *saintly* Nicholas on whom the current sanitized Santa Claus is based—marched across the debate hall and slapped the face of Arius. If it happened, a mild gesture, maybe, compared to such a malicious heresy.

The Church had no time to recuperate from the fractious assault on the nature of the Son of God, for a new struggle was brewing—over the nature of the Holy Spirit. Again, sharp questions pierced the air: Is the Holy Spirit divine? In what sense? Is the Holy Spirit equal with the Son and the Father or more of an impersonal force or energy between those two? If the Son and Holy Spirit are equal with God the Father, then are there, logically, three gods?

Among those churchmen who fought against the equality of the Holy Spirit with the Father were the *pneumatomachians*, or "Spirit-fighters." Macedonius, a bishop of Constantinople who denied the full divinity of the Holy Spirit, fanned their flame of dissension. And once again, the Church was called upon to more firmly establish the content of her faith and restore peace to her children.

Answering that call was, among others, Saint Basil the Great. Like many Church leaders in these turbulent centuries, Saint Basil would have preferred a quieter life. In fact, history remembers Saint Basil as much for his pioneering work in monasticism as for his penetrating writings during the Trinitarian controversy. But Saint Basil felt moved by the very Spirit he was called upon to defend, and, as a bishop, he wanted to see peace and right faith return to the Christian communities. When he surveyed the condition of the Church, he likened it to a naval battle being fought in a raging storm.

His counsel summoned and his conscience moved, Saint Basil wrote a treatise called *On the Holy Spirit*. On display in this work are both Saint Basil's sharp intellect and his pastoral sensitivity. Words matter, he believed, so we had better get our language about God correct. "Those who are idle in the pursuit of righteousness," he wrote of those he considered careless about such things, "count theological terminology as secondary."[8] Much of *On the Holy Spirit* is devoted to the role of prepositions in Holy Scripture.

Words matter because how we understand something influences what we believe about it, and what we believe about it influences our relationship with it. If I believe, for example, that my neighbor is a dangerous criminal, my belief—*right or wrong*—affects how I relate to him. More importantly, my belief about what God is like—*right or wrong*—affects how I relate to Him and how I perceive He relates to me, and that belief spills into the river of faith downstream: prayer life, worship life, and my whole relationship with the divine.

In *On the Holy Spirit*, Saint Basil deftly argues for the full divinity of the Holy Spirit and the Spirit's full equality with the Father and the Son. Since both the truths of God and the souls of men were at stake, he believed, Saint Basil argued for the divinity of the Holy Spirit but avoided using the controversial language that might further isolate his opponents from the Church. Nowhere in *On the Holy Spirit* does Saint Basil write that "the Holy Spirit is God"—a detail that *On the Holy Spirit* shares with Holy Scripture itself, which may explain some of Saint Basil's reticence. Yet the book assembles an enormous record of references to the divinity of the Holy Spirit from the biblical, baptismal, and liturgical tradition of the Church. And that tradition, Saint Basil explains, requires that we give "glory to the Father with the Only-begotten One, and do not exclude the Holy Spirit from this same glory."[9] He continues:

The Holy Spirit partakes of the fullness of divinity.[10]

If wherever God is, the Spirit is present also, what nature shall we presume Him to have?[11]

The Holy Spirit is always described as united with the Godhead; why should He be deprived of His glory?[12]

These fundamental truths are embedded into the worshiping life of the Church through the Divine Liturgy that Saint Basil helped assemble and that bears his name. Just before the bread and wine are shown to be the body and blood of Christ—an act of change accomplished by the Holy Spirit—the priest calls the Holy Spirit "the Spirit of truth, the Gift of adoption, the Pledge of the inheritance to come, the First-fruits of eternal good things, the life-giving Power, the Fountain of Sanctification." And not just bread and wine but worshipers too are changed by this Holy Spirit, "by Whose enabling every rational and intelligent creature doth ascribe to [the Father] perpetual praise."[13]

But in the turbulent fourth century, in which Saint Basil lived, debate stretched beyond the question of *if* the Holy Spirit is God to include the question of *how* the Holy Spirit is God. Critics wondered how those who believed in a shared divinity could escape the charge of polytheism—if the Father and the Son and the Holy Spirit are all divine, then are not all three gods? Such a question provided an opportunity for Church Fathers to articulate a decisive and lasting description of the unity-in-plurality of the Trinity.

By "Church Fathers" here, we mean especially Saint Basil, his friend Saint Gregory the Theologian, and Basil's younger brother, Saint Gregory of Nyssa—three bishops called, because of where they lived, Cappadocian Fathers. (Cappadocia is a region near the center of what is now Turkey, and some of its citizens had been part of the Pentecost event, described in Acts 2.)

The fourth-century Cappadocian Fathers laid a sturdy part of the foundation on which all later Orthodox reflection on the Trinity would rest: the Father and the Son and the Holy Spirit share one divine essence—called *Nature*—while each has a particular existence, or way of being, unique to Him—called *Hypostasis* (which means, "what stands under"). By way of analogy, Saint Basil referred to an idea from Aristotle: every human being is a distinct person who "stands under" the general nature all human beings share in common. "Nature is to person as general is to particular," wrote Saint Basil in a later letter.[14]

So, the godhead is "one essence in three hypostases," or one Nature in three Persons. Or, as Saint Symeon the New Theologian describes the Trinity, "triple light in unity but unique light in three."[15] In the service of Matins on Pentecost morning, we proclaim, "Light is the Father, and Light the Son, and Light the Holy Spirit."[16] Nature does not precede *Hypostasis*, and *Hypostasis* does not precede Nature—this "tri-unity" is a single and simple reality.

Within the Trinity there is *order*—the Father is the cause or source of divinity for the Son and the Holy Spirit—but there is no *inferiority*—the Son and the Holy Spirit are equal with the Father. The God of the Bible, of the Creed, and of the Liturgy, is not the Holy Trinity but the one Father who shares His divinity with the Son and the Holy Spirit. The Son is God, or divine, because He is *of* God the Father; the Holy Spirit is God, or divine, because He is *of* God the Father. Each is distinct but not a distinct god; *God is one* and from His divinity exists a communion of love—Father, Son, and Holy Spirit in one essence, one will, one glory, and "one power, one rank, one worship," as we sing on Pentecost morning.[17] This existence of the three has no beginning and no end. Rather, it is simply a state of being. That is to say, God *is*.

Every touch of God upon His world is Trinitarian—*from* the Father *through* the Son *in* the Holy Spirit.[18] No Person of the Trinity acts independently of the other two. Saint Gregory of Sinai, writing almost a thousand years after the Cappadocians, explains that "God is known and understood in everything in three *hypostases* [or Persons]. He holds all things and provides for all things through His Son, in the Holy Spirit, and no one of them, whenever He is invoked, is named or thought of as existing apart or separately from the other two."[19] Any invocation of the Holy Spirit brings a person into the presence of the Son and the Father too. For within the Godhead, wrote Saint Gregory of Nyssa, is *koinonia*—inseparable communion.[20]

Just as the first ecumenical council had been called, in part, to express the teaching of the Church on the divinity of Christ, the second ecumenical council was called, in part, to express the teaching of the Church on the divinity of the Holy Spirit. This gathering, convened in the city of Constantinople fifty-six years after the first council, also served to fortify the creed—the statement of belief—that had been drafted at the first council. While the first council had included in its creed the simple statement, "We believe in the Holy Spirit," the ensuing five decades of controversy surrounding the divinity of the Holy Spirit required the second council to thicken the creed with *what* Christians believe about the Holy Spirit:

And I believe in the Holy Spirit, the Lord and Giver of Life, who proceeds from the Father, who with the Father and the Son together is worshipped and glorified, who spoke by the prophets.

Saint Basil's style of speaking the truth while attempting to avoid further isolating his opponents—"their loss causes me tears and continual sorrow"[21]—was retained by the Church Fathers of the second ecumenical council. They withheld from the creed the phrase *of one essence* to describe the relationship of the Holy Spirit with the Father that the first council had used to describe the relationship of the Son with the Father. One goal, perhaps, was not to obliterate the opponents but to protect the truth while removing as many stumbling blocks as possible that would keep the opponents from embracing the truth.

From sprout to bloom. Even as the Father and the Son and the Holy Spirit are present in every divine touch on creation, the revelation of the Holy Trinity to humanity's full wonder blossomed over time. This was a measured unveiling—granting to the world what we needed when we needed it—and the work of a God tender toward the souls of all who may believe. As Saint Gregory the Theologian, Basil's friend and co-Cappadocian, wrote:

> The Old Testament clearly showed the Father, but only dimly showed the Son. The New Testament revealed the Son and hinted at the divinity of the Spirit. Today the Spirit lives among us, and is making himself more clearly known. As long as the divinity of the Father had not been recognized, it was dangerous to preach openly the Son; in the same way, as long as the divinity of the Son was not admitted, it was dangerous to impose, if we dare to use such words, the belief in the divinity of the Spirit as an added burden. You see the order in which God is revealed, an order that we must respect in our own turn: not revealing everything in a rush and without discernment but also not keeping anything hidden until the end of time. The one tendency risked injuring those who were outside, and the other one would have separated us from our own brothers.[22]

By the end of the fourth century, the Trinitarian controversies had largely come to a close. Heretical ideas about the Father or the Son or the Holy Spirit would still emerge and cause division, but, with a strong and rooted Trinitarian theology now in place for the Church, these would be considered less of a threat and more of the same: deeply misguided attempts to change or innovate, to add or detract, even to overthink.

The Spirit of the Lord—the *ruah Yahweh*—that descended upon prophets and judges and kings, upon apostles and fathers and saints, is not an impersonal force or divine vibration. He is, as the prayer to Him states, a "heavenly king," the third Person of the Holy Trinity, who shares royalty with the Son that both receive from the Father. As the Vespers of Pentecost proclaims, the Holy Spirit is "equal to the Father in Substance and throne."[23]

That the Holy Spirit is called "king," however, does not tell us what *kind* of King He is. For that, we look to the next part of the prayer, and the next chapter of our story.

2
The Comforter

O heavenly King, the Comforter, the Spirit of truth, Who art
everywhere present and fillest all things; Treasury of good
things and Giver of life; come and abide in us, and cleanse
us from every impurity, and save our souls, O Gracious Lord.

•

SPIRITUAL SEARCHER, afflicted for three
days with what he called "thousands of
savage thoughts, each making its own
demands and giving its own orders,"
went to the Greek monastic peninsula of Mount Athos to seek
consoling from his new friend, the twentieth-century saintly
monk Elder Paisios. "I was so weary," he wrote, "so physically and
spiritually exhausted that I could hardly walk straight." He found
the monk working alone in the yard outside his monastic cell.

Elder Paisios received him warmly and, sensing his guest's
troubled state, asked, "How are your spirits holding up?" "Oh,
Elder," he replied, "I can't continue anymore. I can't take it any
longer." "Have a seat," Elder Paisios said, "so we can put things
in order."

The gentle monk approached the tormented man, reached
out his hand, and tapped him lightly on the head. Suddenly,
everything was different:

The flood of evil thoughts was brought to a halt. But this didn't just bring an end to my suffering. My mind didn't simply return to a normal state, such as it is in as I write these words. No, it entered a deeper, more distant realm, of quiet tranquility, great joy, and profound peace. Another Spirit had been united to my mind and, out of kindness, had freely imparted to me that which was His by nature. I am afraid and ashamed to say it, but perhaps it really was that Person that Christ called the Comforter, for He truly comforted me. It made my trial seem trivial, and I would gladly have suffered another such trial, if it would have meant receiving such consolation.[24]

The Holy Spirit may grace a troubled soul in a thousand different ways, even through a knock on the head by a saint.

Christ never promised His followers a life free from pain or pernicious thoughts. In fact, the promise was much greater: "Behold, I send the Promise of My Father upon you" (Luke 24:49). The promise, then, is a Person, and that Person—the Holy Spirit—would reveal Himself to the troubled soul in a most sublime way: as the Comforter (John 14:16).

Five words into the prayer to the Holy Spirit—"O heavenly King, the Comforter"—and the prayer yields a marvelous treasure: the heavenly King, one of the almighty Godhead, is also the comforting King, the compassionate King, the consoling King. His presence is not aloof or tyrannical, but personal and uplifting.

The Holy Spirit is called the Comforter at a moment when the disciples would soon need comforting. The world is going to hate you, Christ speaks candidly, and I am going to leave you. Yet cradling such troubling news was the assurance that not only would the disciples not be abandoned after Christ's departure but also that His departure would lead to a magnificent arrival. "I will pray the Father," Jesus explains, "and He will give you another [Comforter], that He may abide with you forever." And that Comforter will not linger externally like some mystical vapor in the air, but "He dwells with you and will be in you" (John 14:16–17). The comfort of the Holy Spirit will be an interior glow.

Comforter, as we saw earlier, is *parakletos*, which may be understood as someone who is called or summoned to render care. But care for what? Comfort implies pain, need, the easing of a tension or the soothing of a hurt.

There is a suffering common to all persons—the suffering of simply being alive. If it's not the world around us delivering some measure of burden, it's the world within—"outside were conflicts," admitted Saint Paul, "inside were fears" (2 Cor. 7:5). Even if our bills are paid and our health is strong, anxiety or insecurity or anger or depression provide their own trouble. "Be kind," begins a quotation commonly attributed to the Jewish philosopher Philo of Alexandria, "for everyone you meet is fighting a hard battle."

Everyone. Orthodox Christians do not believe that the comfort of the Holy Spirit is reserved only for the Orthodox in particular or the Christian in general, if by comfort we mean any touch of divine aid that gives a person the strength to simply carry on. At the time he was soothed by the Holy Spirit through the gentle knock on the head by Elder Paisios, the troubled man not only did not claim to be a Christian but had also been exploring witchcraft, yoga, and Hinduism at the time he befriended the monk. As we shall see later in the prayer serving as our narrative guide, the Holy Spirit is "everywhere present and fillest all things." *All things* includes *all flesh*, upon which God promised, through the prophet Joel, that He would pour out His Spirit (Joel 3:1).

But while the prophet announced that the Holy Spirit would be poured out upon everyone, not everyone would be willing to receive Him. Christ, as He assures His disciples that they will be sent "another Comforter," acknowledges that this Comforter is He "whom the world cannot receive, because it neither sees Him nor knows Him" (John 14:16–17).

"World" here suggests *worldliness*. Saint Theophylact of Bulgaria, an eleventh-century biblical commentator, identifies the "world" in these words of Christ in the Gospel of John as "coarse people who think only about physical existence." He writes, " 'Worldly people cannot see the Spirit,' the Lord explains, 'because they lack divine perception, neither can such people know Him.' "

The apostles, however, can know the Spirit, and they represent those who have renounced carnality in favor of spiritual life rooted in the transcendent God. " 'What makes you able to know the Holy Spirit and receive Him?' Christ asks. 'The fact that you are not of this world.' "[25]

We might say, therefore, that the comfort of the Holy Spirit is received by everyone as either an *external aid* or an *internal experience.* Notice the words of the apostle John in the prologue of the Gospel that bears his name:

> [Christ] was in the world, and the world was made through Him, and the world did not know Him. He came to His own, and His own did not receive Him. But as many as received Him, to them He gave the right to become children of God, to those who believe in His name. (John 1:10–12)

Every human being is a *creation* of God, but not every human being is a *child* of God. As God's creation, every person is imbued with transcendence and deserves profound respect and care, especially the "least of these" in whom Christ especially dwells (Matt. 25:31–46). Still, the distinction remains. And the process from being a creation of God to becoming a child of God, according to the apostle John, involves receiving and believing in Jesus Christ: "As many as *received* Him, to them He gave the right to become children of God, to those who *believe* in His name."

So, with the Christ comes the comfort of the Holy Spirit, and with the comfort of the Holy Spirit comes the Christ. The Trinity is inseparable. Remember those Church Fathers who struggled to articulate the reality of the Trinity? They described three distinct Persons—Father, Son, Holy Spirit—united in a single Nature—one God.

Because the Holy Spirit does not act independently of the other Persons of the Trinity, we cannot embrace the Holy Spirit while rejecting the Son. The apostle Paul even describes the Holy Spirit as the "Spirit of Christ" (Rom. 8:9). Further emphasizing the unity of the Son and the Spirit in his reflection on Pentecost, Saint Gregory Palamas, archbishop of Thessalonica in the fourteenth century, asks, "Why did the Holy Spirit appear in the form of tongues? It was to demonstrate that He shared the same nature as the Word of God, for there is no relationship closer than that between word and tongue."[26]

If, as Christ teaches in the Gospel of John, a person "of the world" cannot receive the Holy Spirit, it is because there has been no fundamental transformation from *creation* of God to *child* of God—a change possible only *in Christ*. The grace of God pours forth everywhere and upon all yet changes only the willing. Water moves over the surface of hard soil, but moving on soft, it penetrates within.

The *creation* of God will receive the comfort of the Holy Spirit as an external aid—as grace sprinkled like mist through life in ways numberless and known only to the God who loves all and without partiality. But the *child* of God will receive that comfort as an internal experience—as grace indwelling the deep heart and affecting transformation from within. One *receives* light, which he or she may not even notice, while the other *becomes* light.

The transformation from a creation of God to a child of God is a glorious but messy process, as our old nature fights to the death and our new nature struggles to emerge. Old habits or ways of thinking, once so natural and familiar, are exposed by the Holy Spirit—now acting within a person—as unworthy of this new calling. Through a thousand tiny deaths and births, the whole of a person—spirit, body, mind—undergoes change. The old, fragmented, conflicted creation becomes, gradually, the new, integrated, whole child. And this process involves a sacred kind of pain.

Christ's reference to the Holy Spirit as Comforter is part of a longer narrative in which Christ also reveals that this Comforter "will convict the world of sin, and of righteousness, and of judgment" (John 16:8). The Comforter convicts, so the pain He comes to soothe is often a pain He Himself inflicts. The Comforter, as the prayer to the Holy Spirit reveals, is also the Spirit of truth: He uncovers, reveals, exposes. Because He *is* light, He brings things *to* light.

The Holy Spirit in the Orthodox tradition cannot be limited to some kind of soothing cosmic nurse who exists only to make people feel better. He restores, yes, but also chastens, and both restoration and chastening are proofs of His love. "Whom the Lord loves, He instructs, and chastises every son He receives" (Prov. 3:12). The growth of a person from being God's creation toward becoming His child involves struggle as the Holy Spirit reveals and uproots the manifold imperfections within us. This purifying struggle brings pain but also invites the comfort necessary to keep going.

Chastening and comfort are two hands with which God fashions new children out of old creations. Apparently, He has dealt with His children this way for a long time.

When Moses brought the Hebrews to the threshold of the Promised Land, he reminded them of their relationship with the living God, a relationship that involved both blessing and correction. "You should know in your heart that as a man chastens his son," Moses told the children of God, "so the Lord your God chastens you." He goes on:

> Therefore, you shall keep the commandments of the Lord your God to walk in His ways and to fear Him. For the Lord your God is bringing you into a good and great land, where torrents of waters and springs of bottomless depths flow through the plains and through the mountains; a land of wheat and barley, of vines, fig trees, and pomegranates, a land of olive oil and honey; a land where you will not eat your bread in poverty, and in which you will lack nothing." (Deut. 8:5–9)

The Hebrew people were not without sin, but even without sin to uproot, the hands of the Holy Spirit are not entirely mild. "I assure you," wrote Saint Macarius the Great, a fourth-century Desert Father, "that even the Apostles, though they had the Comforter, were not entirely without anxiety. With joy and gladness they had fear and trembling, *proceeding from grace itself, not from the side of evil*; but the same grace secured them, that they might not swerve, though it were but a little."[27]

The Holy Spirit is the sculptor who beautifies the marble of the heart with sharp strokes but does not leave us with the pain that comes as the imperfections fall. "The Savior and the Comforter," wrote Saint John of Kronstadt, a Russian priest of the nineteenth century, "two Persons of the Godhead: the One ever saves from sins, the Other comforts him who is saved. Their very names are taken from their deeds."[28]

The sculpting by the Holy Spirit is one part of this purification process; the other rests with the marble. The Holy Spirit falls upon both the creation of God and the child of God. But everyone—child or not—must choose what to do with that grace of purification when it comes. We can cooperate or we can resist. And here we discover a frailty we all have in common.

In the Gospels, Jesus engages suffering persons with what appears to be a strange question: "Do you want to be healed?" This appears strange because it appears to have an obvious answer. Would the suffering have asked for healing if they did not want it? Who doesn't want healing? Who doesn't want comfort? As it turns out, many of us.

Our approach to becoming spiritually well may resemble the way we take medication to ease physical pain rather than look to the cause of that pain. We take pain medication because we want to feel better. However, what if the real problem is not in how the body feels but in how the body *is*? When we feel pain, we swallow a pill to make the pain go away. This is called *relief*. But if the pain is symptomatic of a more serious health issue, the goal is no longer only the easing of pain but tracing the pain to its root and dealing with that deeper issue. This is called *healing*.

Relief or healing. This is the choice of all who seek deliverance from physical, and spiritual, affliction. The bitter pain of resentment, for example, can be an ailment from which we wish to be delivered, but we must decide whether we want the quick relief that, say, self-justification brings, or the lasting healing from, perhaps, the disease of pride toward which the resentment may point. Depression, irritability, anger, anxiety, fear—these can all be ailments from which we wish to be delivered, but we must choose either quick relief from the pain they bring or lasting healing from a possibly deeper disease. And yes, we decide. When the grace of God comes, it does not overwhelm the will that chooses how far to let it penetrate. The patient must cooperate with the Physician.

And every patient is unique. When we looked at *Hypostasis* in chapter 1, we discovered that each human being is distinct and "stands under" the general human nature we all share. So, not only does each person suffer from a brokenness particular to him or her; but each will also experience the comfort of the Holy Spirit in ways equally particular. Grace for all yet unique to each—the Divine Liturgy holds this balance when, as the baptized faithful are drawing near for Holy Communion, the priest prays that the Lord Himself "will distribute these gifts here spread forth, *unto all of us for good, according to the individual need of each.*"[29]

We can try to describe what "comfort" means—peace, presence, strength, contentment, support, reassurance, solace, encouragement, grace—but we cannot measure the countless ways comfort is received and experienced by humanity. We see the tapestry of God's movement in the world from beneath, with its often-incomprehensible tangle of threads; only God sees the tapestry with its beautiful design from above.

Every human being is created to be in communion with God—whole, complete, at peace—for this is our natural state. God's every touch upon the world is designed toward that end. The transformation called for within us is not occasional and cosmetic but permanent and thorough. The comfort of the

Holy Spirit is deep medicine designed to restore a person "to the measure of the stature of the fullness of Christ" (Eph. 4:13). This comfort is designed, as all things with God, to prepare the soul for eternity.

From shadow to light, promise to fulfillment, race to prize—these are biblical analogies of the relationship of life on earth to eternity with God. The comfort of the Holy Spirit soothes the troubled soul with a foretaste of—as we Orthodox say in our prayers for the departed, referring to the words of the prophet Isaiah and found later in Revelation—"a place of brightness, a place of repose, where all sickness, sorrow, and sighing have fled away" (Isa. 35:10; Rev. 21:4). To receive such comfort is like catching the scent of paradise.

"How can one feel truly comforted," asks Elder Paisios, "if he does not believe in God and in true and eternal life after death? When man grasps the deeper meaning of this true life, stress goes away, divine consolation comes, and he is healed."[30]

3
The Spirit of Truth

O heavenly King, the Comforter, the Spirit of truth, Who art
everywhere present and fillest all things; Treasury of good
things and Giver of life; come and abide in us, and cleanse
us from every impurity, and save our souls, O Gracious Lord.

•

A GROUP OF SCHOOLCHILDREN ages six and
seven were meeting with Sister Magdalen, a
contemporary Orthodox nun, at a convent
in England. The kindly nun was helping the
children understand the meaning of the word *Orthodox*. One
meaning, Sister Magdalen explained, is "right worship." One
child exclaimed, "We worship in school and sing songs about
God. There's one that goes . . ." and the rest of the children
added their voices to the tune.

"It is nice music," the nun replied. "You must have nice schools
if you learn songs about God." Sister Magdalen noticed a line in
the children's song—"the creed doesn't matter"—and referred
to it when speaking about the importance not only of believing
but also of *what* one believes.

What is a creed? the children wanted to know.

"When we say, 'I believe,' " Sister Magdalen replied. "When you're a baby your godmother says it for you but now you're all old enough to say 'I believe.' It *does* matter what you say about Jesus Christ and who He is. If you say the wrong creed it's like saying lies about God. If we don't say right things it's like having a bad drawing of God and you can't find Him."[31]

True soul work within a person involves discarding any bad drawings of God we may have acquired in the search for the real thing. For some atheists, the God they do not believe in is simply a collection of bad drawings they have picked up over the years—the Merciless Tyrant, for example, or the Cosmic Killjoy. The believer who has bathed in the mercy and joy of the true God shares with the atheist an unbelief in that kind of deity.

The creed to which the nun was referring is recited by Orthodox Christians at every Divine Liturgy. It's a good drawing of God. As we learned in chapter 2, Christians of antiquity convened councils as a way to sift through competing truth claims, and the first two councils drafted the "Nicene-Constantinopolitan" Creed, which the Orthodox have embraced ever since. From the Latin term *credo*—"I believe"—the creed is our statement of what we believe to be true.

Reading through the creed together, we can consider what it reveals about the Holy Spirit, who is the "Spirit of truth," as Christ calls Him in the Gospel of John (14:17; 15:26; 16:13), and about the Godhead in which He dwells:

I believe in one God, the Father Almighty, Maker of heaven and earth, and of all things visible and invisible;

And in one Lord Jesus Christ, the Son of God, the Only-begotten, Begotten of the Father before all worlds, Light of Light, Very God of Very God, Begotten, not made; of one essence with the Father; by Whom all things were made:

Who for us men and for our salvation came down from heaven, and was incarnate of the Holy Spirit and the Virgin Mary, and became man;

And was crucified also for us under Pontius Pilate, and suffered and was buried;

And the third day He rose again, according to the Scriptures;

And ascended into heaven, and sits at the right hand of the Father;

And He shall come again with glory to judge the living and the dead, Whose kingdom shall have no end.

And I believe in the Holy Spirit, the Lord, and Giver of life, Who proceeds from the Father, Who with the Father and the Son together is worshipped and glorified, Who spake by the prophets;

And I believe in One Holy Catholic Apostolic Church;

I acknowledge one Baptism for the remission of sins;

I look for the Resurrection of the dead,

And the Life of the world to come. Amen.

In both pronounced and subtle ways, the Holy Spirit is present throughout the creed. First, notice that the creed clearly describes what Orthodox Christians believe about the Holy Spirit:

And I believe in the Holy Spirit, the Lord, and Giver of Life, Who proceeds from the Father, Who with the Father and the Son together is worshipped and glorified, Who spake by the prophets.

This "Spirit of truth" is called "Lord" and "Giver of Life." His divinity is grounded in the Father alone, from whom He alone "proceeds," and He is "worshipped and glorified" with the Father and the Son. He "spake by the prophets," showing that He was active in the world long before the Christ child took residence in the womb of the Virgin—the same Virgin who cooperated with the Holy Spirit to bring about the Incarnation. These are the simple and straightforward truths in the creed that the children conversing with the nun at the convent could easily grasp.

Beneath the surface of the creed, however, swim more subtle revelations about this "Spirit of truth." The reference in the creed to the Holy Spirit was drafted at the second ecumenical council, decades after the references to the Father and the Son had been drafted at the first ecumenical council. And yet the Spirit was mystically present in the creed from the very beginning.

"Because you are sons, God has sent forth the Spirit of His Son into your hearts, crying out, 'Abba, Father!' " (Gal. 4:6). The person in whom the Holy Spirit is present will call upon God, as the creed does in its opening sentence, as *Father*. God is our Father—our Source, our Beginning, He who initiates—and by the name Father is He known. "There is, and always will be, an ontological distance between God, Who is unconditional Primordial Being, and man, who is His creation," wrote the twentieth century Orthodox priest and monk Father Sophrony Sakharov. "But in the Act of creation 'in His image, after His likeness,' our Creator in effect repeats Himself, and in this sense is our Father."[32]

This choice of words in the creed is important. To call upon the Trinity as, for example, "Creator, Redeemer, Sanctifier," is not the same as calling upon the Trinity as "Father, Son, Holy Spirit." The former describe *actions*—they address God as He exists in relation to us; the latter are names of *being*—they address God as He exists within Himself. Orthodox prayers are filled with references to "Father, Son, and Holy Spirit" because we strive to come to God on what we understand to be His terms, as Who He Is in Himself—the great "I AM" (Exod. 3:14). This understanding of God's being above creation, rather than merely His role in creation, is crucial if the goal of human life is to transcend this fallen world that is "passing away" (1 John 2:17) and become "partakers of the divine nature" (2 Pet. 1:4).

Scripture shows, then, that the drafters of the Nicene Creed and those who recite it can call upon God as *Father* in a meaningful way because "Father" is inspired by the Holy Spirit. So the creed's first subtle revelation of the Spirit of truth involves the first Person of the Trinity—the Father. In reflecting on a conversation she had with a four-year-old girl who called upon God as "Daddy," Sister Magdalen writes, "From childhood we relate to God in this way. Indeed, to relate to Him like this is the criterion of a true relationship. 'Unless you become like children' (Matthew 18:3)."[33]

A second subtle revelation the creed offers about the Holy Spirit involves the second Person of the Trinity—the Son. "No one can say that Jesus is Lord except by the Holy Spirit" (1 Cor. 12:3). In addition to calling upon God as Father, the soul in whom the Holy Spirit is active will also call, as the creed does in its reference to Him, upon Jesus as *Lord*.

Jesus of Nazareth is an object of interest for some people, an object of worship for others. For those inspired by the Holy Spirit, He is both. They read, they study, they consider His life even as they follow, adore, and submit to Him as Lord. The Nicene Creed contains a reference to Pontius Pilate, the Roman governor who presided over the crucifixion of Christ. It's a sudden shot of history in a document of theology, but it grounds the creed's eternal truths in the soil of time and place.

Early non-Christian figures—such as Josephus, a Jewish historian who wrote about the crucifixion, or Tacitus, a Roman historian who wrote about Nero's hatred for Christians and their "Christus," or Pliny the Younger, a Roman senator who wrote about persecuting Christians who refused to renounce Christ—testify to the existence of Jesus of Nazareth; but they are certainly not Matthew or Mark or Luke. The reference to Christ in the creed is, as are the Gospels themselves, an *interpretation* inspired by the Holy Spirit of who Jesus of Nazareth is—the Lord of history, the Lord of eternity, the Lord of lords. And *who Christ is* also describes *what Christ does*—the Son of God became the Son of Man so that the sons of men might become sons of God.

The Holy Spirit opens our eyes to behold the lordship, indeed, the whole magnificence of Christ. Christ is Lord, the Spirit reveals, because Christ is *Logos*—the *Word* of God. Inspired by the Holy Spirit, the apostle John wrote, "In the beginning was the *Logos*, and the *Logos* was with God, and the *Logos* was God. . . . All things were made through Him, and without Him nothing was made that was made" (John 1:1, 3).

The term *Logos* first appears six centuries before Christ, but both Holy Scripture and the Church of the first three centuries after Christ use the term in its original, *personal* sense: "Venerate this crib," wrote Saint Gregory the Theologian in his fourth-century *Homilies on Christmas*, "because from it you who were deprived of meaning are fed by the divine Meaning, the divine Logos Himself."[34]

Originally, *Logos* meant "word, reason, inherent structure, creative pattern, ordering principle." But the biblical and patristic vision connects the term with the Person of the Son of God, so Christ was proclaimed to be the *word* and *reason* and *inherent structure* of creation. Holy Scripture reveals the magnificent depth of the *Logos*—this Word creates, this Word is enshrined in the Law of Moses, this Word visits the Prophets, this Word inspires the Psalms (see Luke 24:44), this Word sent forth from God does not return to Him empty (Isa. 55:10–11). And notice how the apostle Paul speaks of the centrality of this Word to all things:

For by [Christ] all things were created that are in heaven
and that are on earth, visible and invisible, whether thrones
or dominions or principalities or powers. All things were
created through Him and for Him. And He is before all
things, and in Him all things consist. (Col. 1:16–17)

Creation by itself can only tell us that there is a Creator. It
does not tell us who or what that Creator is, its nature or char-
acter, or why creation was made. For that, we turn to the "Spirit
of truth," who reveals the *Logos of* creation to be the *Lord over*
creation. The Orthodox vision of the world may be described
as "seeing all things in Christ and Christ in all things." As a
person acquires the Holy Spirit the faculties of perception are
cleansed, and he or she feels the Spirit within drawing toward
the holy *Logos*, just as "deep calls to deep" (Ps. 40:7).

Crafted under the guidance of the Holy Spirit, the Nicene
Creed calls upon God as *Father* and upon Jesus as *Lord*. These,
we believe, are foundational truths about the Godhead, and the
validity of all claims about what the Holy Spirit reveals of God
may be judged against them.

The revelations brought by "the Spirit of truth," however,
do not end with the Father and the Son. The Holy Spirit also
reveals the truth about two other important realities that will
never pass away: the human being and the Church.

To burn away all misperceptions about ourselves until all that
remains is God's vision of us—nothing more and nothing less—
this is the work of the Holy Spirit. And that vision is breath-
taking. The Desert Father Saint Macarius the Great reflects on
God's limitless love for humanity. He imagines a kind of sacred

dance between God, the masculine who initiates, and the soul, the feminine who responds. They are distinct in essence but united in love. "He is God and she is non-God," Saint Macarius writes:

> He is the Lord, and she, the handmaid; He, the Creator, and she, the creation; He, the Architect, and she, the fabric; and there is nothing in common between Him and her nature. But by means of His infinite and ineffable and incomprehensible love and compassion, it pleased Him to make His indwelling in this made thing.[35]

God is *pleased* to dwell within the human being. The simple acceptance of that truth is a monumental victory, a sacred moment, a transformative epiphany, a life-changer. The gods of pagan antiquity created the universe from an act of violence and, as an afterthought, made humanity as caretaker and slave. The God of Judeo-Christianity, however, created the world *on purpose* and, in His own Image, made humanity as its finest expression. But this is a truth we cannot assimilate into ourselves on our own. It is a revelation that, like all illumination, is a gift of the Holy Spirit.

In Orthodox thought, the spiritual person is not merely a person with a soul or a person who has developed any number of "energies" of the soul—emotion, for example, or reason or creativity. This is why words like *spirituality* need careful definition. "The word *spirituality* can suggest a purely psychological analysis of feelings, attitudes, and religious behavior without any reference to the object sought after by the believing person," wrote the modern writer Elisabeth Behr-Sigel. "We believe it is impossible to separate spirituality from the content of the faith."[36]

The spiritual person, then, is the one in whom the Holy Spirit dwells and to whom the Spirit reveals. Within the spiritual person are found no lies or delusion, only truth with a sense of belonging; he knows who he is and to Whom he belongs. "In the hearts of the saints," wrote Saint Silouan, a Russian monk who lived on the Greek peninsula of Mount Athos and who died in 1938, "lives the grace of the Holy Spirit, making them kin with God, and they feel without a doubt that they are spiritual children of the Heavenly Father."[37]

This relationship between truth and our sense of self lies at the heart of many spiritual struggles. We struggle when we view ourselves not through the lens of pure truth but through, for example, the lens of emotion—we lose our proper orientation when we automatically believe that what our emotions are telling us at any given moment is the truth. Emotions are so powerful that we may be tempted to believe they always reflect reality as it really is.

The Orthodox spiritual tradition has been helping with this problem for a long time. Saints through the ages have explored the relationship between truth and perception, between how God sees us and how we see ourselves. As we consider what they have to offer, it is important to know that Orthodox Christians profess a *traditional conviction* about the devil—that he is real.

The saints tell us that one of the devil's strategies is to whisper *half-truths* into our minds, thoughts like: you're worthless; God cannot forgive you for what you've done; no one likes you;

you're a fraud. These are half-truths because there is something true in them: yes, compared to Christ who is perfect in every way, I am worthless; yes, I have and continue to defile myself before the righteous God; yes, sometimes I am not liked and sometimes I do not live what I believe.

Other half-truths whispered to us, still from the devil, can be positive in nature: you're the best person you know; stop trying so hard, you're salvation is already secure; a little sin is okay; everyone loves you; you're always in the right. Again, these are half-truths because there is something true in them: yes, I have a value too great to be described; yes, salvation is a gift that cannot be bartered for with good works; yes, sometimes people act favorably toward me and sometimes I've done the right thing.

So our minds wrap around these half-truths—sometimes negative, sometimes positive—and block everything else out. Then, like the tail on a kite, our emotions follow: we slip toward despair, anger, frustration, or toward vanity, smugness, complacency. The half-truth stirs up the emotions, and we believe that what our emotions are telling us is the whole truth. If this process goes unchecked, we end up in either the depths of depression or the heights of pride—which, actually, is often the same place. In truth, however, we have only believed a lie of the devil. Those lies lead to wrong beliefs about God, about ourselves, and they lead to strained or broken relationships— devastating consequences from some idea that was not true to begin with.

One man, a faithful, committed Christian, unexpectedly fell into a deep depression. He spent long anguished periods in the fetal position, often unable to even get out of bed. His darkening thoughts twisted around profound regrets and seizing self-doubt. When he finally emerged from his misery and was clearheaded, he wrote down a list of lies of the devil he had been believing. He counted fifty-four of them, and the first one on his list was: it is too late.

As he later reflected on his struggle, he came to believe that a person can usually determine the source of thoughts by discerning the *tone of voice* behind them: if a thought is dark and accusatory, if it leads us to question our value or the motives of other persons, or what we know is true about our Lord, a person can be fairly sure that thought comes from the evil one. If a thought leads us toward Christ and His Church, if it leads us to hold other persons more dear, if it leads to an act of light or love or to a fresh appreciation for divine mercy that overwhelms all failure and sin, a person can be fairly sure that thought comes from God.

One way, then, to fight the half-truths of the devil is with the other half of the truth he won't tell us. Only the "Spirit of truth" offers the whole truth about the human person. This is why the pursuit of a vibrant spiritual life is important, because neither our fallen nature nor our simple natural selves "receive the things of the Spirit of God, for they are foolishness to him; nor can he know them, because they are spiritually discerned" (1 Cor. 2:14).

For the Orthodox Christian, that spiritual life will organically unfold within the Ark of Salvation, the Church—that other eternal reality whose glory is revealed and preserved by the Holy Spirit.

To read through the New Testament is to behold, in one sense, the photograph of a baby. We see the Church not in a state of realized fullness, as if it were suddenly birthed into perfect maturity, but with its perfection in germinal form. If the Church is the "body of Christ" (1 Cor. 12:27) and if the Christ child "increased in wisdom and stature, and in favor with God and men" (Luke 2:52), then we can accept that the Church after Pentecost *also* increased in wisdom and stature, and in favor with God and men.

In his book *Credo*, the contemporary Church historian Jaroslav Pelikan calls this increase not *change* but *continuity*.[38] As time passes, the Church does not grow more and more into something it was not intended to be, but more and more into something it already is—what Saint Paul calls "the pillar and ground of the truth" (1 Tim. 3:15) and "the fullness of Him who fills all in all" (Eph. 1:23). The acorn of New Testament faith and practice grows into the vibrant oak tree providing shade for the world with missions and evangelism, saints and martyrs, sacraments and councils, grace and truth. Acorns *continue* as oak trees; they do not *change* into giraffes—every development of Christendom in history may be understood as either another growth in continuity, or a new detour into change.

This continuity can also be called *Holy Tradition*, which may be understood as the life of the Holy Spirit within the Church. Orthodox loyalty is not to the New Testament era, as some static ideal to which the Church must return, but to the Holy Spirit as the inspiration for where the Church must go. Guided by the Holy Spirit, the fullness of the Church remains fixed while some expressions of the Church in space and time remain fluid so that her fullness is always given the best conditions to emerge.

This life of the Holy Spirit within the Church is why the Church could decide not to continue some practices that had been considered useful in the New Testament era but not as useful after—married bishops like the apostle Peter, for example, or restricted meals for converts as in Acts 15. The gift of speaking in tongues—whether the public gift of miraculously preaching the Gospel in languages not one's own as at Pentecost, or the private gift of vocal expressions intelligible to no one but God alone as in Corinth—has generally fallen into disuse among the Orthodox.

Those who profess a belief in the guiding hand of the Holy Spirit are not scandalized by the Church's adjustment of its practices over time, for we know that each adjustment only served to increase her in wisdom and stature, and in favor with God and men.

Father, Son, Human, Church—the truths of these eternal transcendent realities are revealed to the world and preserved by the Holy Spirit, the "Spirit of truth." Lasting expressions of Christian truth, such as the creed, are like lighthouses—they always provide us with proper orientation, with direction in darkness and safety in storm. The creed also expresses our deepest yearning: this really is how we want the important things to be. But as with any other sacred text, reciting the creed frequently must not lead to reciting it thoughtlessly.

Sister Magdalen, at her convent in England, had been discussing the creed with a group of visitors. A teenager said, "But it's boring to say things the same way every time."

"Don't you think," she asked, " 'old' phrases like 'I love you' can still be full of meaning in any age? Or is it boring that people have been saying that for centuries?!"

"Granted," the teenager replied, "but how can I say the Creed with as much meaning as I'd put into telling someone I love them?"

Sister Magdalen said, "You're right. It should have that personal content. That's probably why we say 'I believe' even when we're together and even though the fact that 'we believe' is important too. Maybe we can pray inside that we'll see for ourselves one day the truth of what we're reciting. Perhaps God does not need to hear us say the Creed, but we need to remind ourselves of the facts we base our life on."[39]

4
Who Art Everywhere Present and Fillest All Things

O heavenly King, the Comforter, the Spirit of truth, Who art
everywhere present and fillest all things; Treasury of good
things and Giver of life; come and abide in us, and cleanse
us from every impurity, and save our souls, O Gracious Lord.

•

I KNOW THAT GOD IS EVERYWHERE," wrote Saint John
Chrysostom, the late-fourth-century bishop of
Constantinople, "and I know that He is everywhere in His whole being. But I do not know
how He is everywhere. I know that He is eternal and has no
beginning. But I do not know how."[40]

Such humility in the face of such mystery is honorable. God
is accessible because He has made Himself so, yet He is also
utterly beyond any idea or concept we could hold of Him. Even
as we say with the Apostle John that "God is love" (1 John 4:8),
we also say that God is totally beyond all our definitions and
categories of love. As one early Church figure wrote, "God cannot be grasped by the mind. If He could be grasped, He would
not be God."[41] So humans are better suited to experience God
than to explain Him. And even when describing our experience

we are cautious, lest what emerges from our description of God is something other than God.

Saint John Chrysostom writes from within a Christian tradition that embraces *antinomy*. An antinomy is an acceptable contradiction between two beliefs or conclusions that are in themselves true. For example, God is *immanent*—everywhere present, filling all things, closer to us than even our own heartbeat. But God is also *transcendent*—nowhere present, above all things, inaccessible to everyone. Each of these contradicts the other, but both are true and the contradiction is true.

Christian faith accepts antinomies: God is one and God is three; Christ is fully God and Christ is fully Man; God foreknows all things and humans have free will; we are saved by our faith and saved by God's grace; we must lose our life to save our life; the cross is an occasion for sorrow and the cross is an occasion for joy; Mary is Mother and Mary is Virgin. Antinomies help shake the mind loose from a strictly logical approach to God, as though God were a concept to be explained rather than a presence to be experienced. These antinomies, however, must not be stretched too far: the truths within them are not opposing or confusing forces, but, rather, distinct elements of one living Divine Reality.

This part of the prayer to the Holy Spirit, who "is everywhere present and fillest all things," speaks of the immanence of God. Orthodox Christianity teaches that while God is transcendent and unknowable in His essence, He is immanent and present in our world in an innermost way—as the personal source and binding force of everything that is, from the Milky Way to the molecule.

The Divine Liturgy affirms that it is God "who didst bring us from non-existence into being."[42] We affirm that not only does everything that has being have God as its source but also that, because God is good, everything is fundamentally good. Or, to use the inspired words of Genesis, "very good" (1:31). Creation, as described in the first chapter of Genesis, is not value-neutral. As Solomon writes, "From the greatness and beauty of created things, the Creator is seen by analogy" (Wisd. 13:5), "for the Creator of beauty created them" (Wisd. 13:3). We are careful, however, not to elevate this principle of analogy too far—the world is not a window to the Creator but closer to a hint.

To approach this mystery of the Holy Spirit, who is "everywhere present and fillest all things," we begin with an Orthodox Christian perspective of creation. As the Nicene Creed states, we believe in "one God, the Father Almighty, Maker of heaven and earth, and of all things visible and invisible," Who created the world out of nothing—creation *ex nihilo*. The mother of the Maccabean martyrs, traditionally called Solomonia, instructs her son to "look at heaven and earth and see everything in them, and know that God made them out of nothing" (2 Macc. 7:28). Before creation, God alone *exists*. His is a perfect, free, complete, independent, uncreated state of being. There was no "raw material" for creation that existed outside of God, so creation emerged from what contemporary writer Philip Sherrard calls "a realm of divine interiority."[43]

Divine interior emphatically does *not* mean divine essence, which is unknowable and inaccessible and entirely independent from all that is created. Instead, divine interior may mean that God fashioned creation from what Church Fathers have called

His *energies*—energies that flow from God, entirely separate yet somehow inseparable from His essence. This is how human beings can know the unknowable God: we cannot know His uncreated essence, yet He condescends to reveal Himself by His uncreated energies. The twentieth-century writer Vladimir Lossky calls this "the antinomy of the accessibility of the inaccessible nature."[44] It's the deep mystery of the Incarnation: the God who is completely other and above all being is born from a womb and lies in a manger.

Saint Maximus the Confessor, a monk and scholar of the seventh century, tells us that this antinomy of the immanence and transcendence of God is closer to us than we realize. In fact, it's part of the central mystery of life itself. His thinking challenges us to stretch our own:

> All immortal things and immortality itself, all living things and life itself, all holy things and holiness itself, all good things and goodness itself, all blessings and blessedness itself, all beings and being itself, are manifestly works of God. Some things began to be in time, for they have not always existed. Others did not begin to be in time, for goodness, blessedness, holiness, and immortality have always existed.[45]

We may understand Saint Maximus to mean that goodness, blessedness, holiness, and immortality are among the uncreated energies of God, and from those energies God has fashioned good and blessed and holy and immortal *and created* things. Contemporary writer Olivier Clément describes this penetrating presence of the Holy Trinity in lovely imagery:

Grace penetrates all things as they tremble and resonate and awaken in this tremendous Breath of life, like a tree in the wind, with sweeping, invisible strokes, like the ocean with its thousands of smiling ripples, or the impulse that moves man and woman toward one another. . . . In his Epistle to the Ephesians (4:6), Paul speaks of God as being above all and through all and in all. It is true that the Father is always the transcendent God, the principle of all reality. The Word is the *Logos* who orders the world through His creative ideas/will. And the Spirit is truly God in all things, enlivening and leading all things to their ultimate fulfillment in beauty. He is the winged God, so represented through symbols of movement and flight: the wind, a bird, the living water; not earth but rather He who makes the earth into a sacrament.[46]

So this antinomy of the immanence and the transcendence of the one living Divine Reality lingers at the silent center of the most pure experiences in human life. It is central, yet always beyond our reach. The bubbling of a mountain stream, simple yet nourishing; the clean whisper of falling snow in the night forest; the sleeping infant, defenseless yet overpowering; the deep energy shared between two persons with walls lowered enough to love—these are the kinds of experiences that, when received at a perfect and often unscripted moment by those open to what they have to give, have stirred poets to rhapsodize and lovers to sing. And yet, poets and lovers, painfully aware of the impermanence of experience, yearn for whatever these experiences point toward—something no longer fleeting, but permanent and unchanging and simply good. Something, or *Someone*. There grows within us a sacred frustration as we approach the essence-energies distinction in God: we feel God in our insatiable desire for more of Him.

Mystics of various religious traditions speak of the translucence of here and now, as if the eternal God uses temporal life to tug at our inner attention. It was written of the saintly nineteenth-century Russian ascetic Anastasia Logacheva, very much a product of her time and place, that, "like many mystics, she lived in two time zones, the present and the eternal. In the present and the temporal, she was a humble peasant woman subject to the usual constraints of her gender and class. In the eternal, she experienced mystical union with the divine and radiated a charismatic authority that drew followers—rich and poor, male and female—to her."[47]

Anastasia's "dual citizenship" of eternity and time, heaven and earth, helps us to understand how the Holy Spirit, while wholly other and beyond, is also "everywhere present and fillest all things." Only God can be absent from all that exists while alive in everything that is. Present even in those persons who deny His existence is the God who has given them being. And while human beings can degenerate into a flurry of sinfulness, even becoming monstrous or mad, they cannot eradicate the goodness at their core. That core is the image of a good God, in whom "we live and move and have our being" (Acts 17:28).

"Everything that breathes," wrote the Russian priest Saint John of Kronstadt, "breathes by air and cannot live without air; similarly, all reasonable free creatures live by the Holy Spirit, as though by air, and cannot live without Him. Recognize that the Holy Spirit stands in the same relation to your soul as air stands in relation to your body."[48]

Our yearning and His nearness—these reveal the imminence of God and His astonishing availability to the world He made. But we do not say He is *only* immanent. To lean toward either the immanence or the transcendence of God to the exclusion of the other is to court error, even grave spiritual harm. So with the saints we fall prostrate before the antinomy that we feel but cannot understand—the nearness of the distant God. Saint Gregory Palamas describes the transcendence of the Holy Spirit with a pen that moves under His very inspiration:

He is not just everywhere, but also above all, not just in every age and time, but before them all. And, according to the promise, the Holy Spirit will not just be with us until the end of the age, but rather will stay with those who are worthy in the age to come, making them immortal and filling their bodies as well with eternal glory, as the Lord indicated by telling His disciples, "I will pray the Father, and He shall give you another Comforter, that He may abide with you forever."[49]

In one fluid phrase, the prayer to the Holy Spirit calls upon Him as the "Spirit of truth, Who art everywhere present and fillest all things." Because, as Saint Gregory says, the Holy Spirit is "not just everywhere, but also above all, not just in every age and time, but before them all," we may also say that His truth is "not just everywhere, but above all, not just in every age and time, but before them all."

Truth, because it belongs to the Spirit, who fills "all things," may emerge beyond the rigid categories into which a person may be accustomed to place it. Life in God is like being in motion while at rest: one can be completely settled in the eternal truths of God while still searching for them. Truth is right doctrine *and* right desire; it is the substance of worthy belief *and* the struggle worthy of blessing. And sometimes it appears in places beyond the familiar horizons.

In the Gospel of Mark, for example, a Jewish scribe approaches Jesus. "Which is the first commandment of all?" he asks the Lord. After Christ's response—a quotation from the prophet Moses about loving God and neighbor—the scribe replies: "Well said, Teacher. You have spoken the truth, for there is one God, and there is no other but He. And to love Him with all the heart, with all the understanding, with all the soul, and with all the strength, and to love one's neighbor as oneself, is more than all the whole burnt offerings and sacrifices." The scribe's confession was wise and true, but incomplete, since he had yet to recognize in the Christ before Him the "one God" he had always worshiped. Jesus replies, "You are not far from the kingdom of God" (Mark 12:28–34).

Not far—that's a measure of distance or degree. Everything outside the visible expressions of the Christian Church cannot be undifferentiated darkness, for the Spirit of truth is "everywhere present and fillest all things." Genuine yearning for God, for truth, for beauty, for peace, for love, for justice—the kind of yearning that consumes a person and organizes one's priorities—may render a person "not far from the kingdom of God." God appears to honor any genuine striving toward Him, peering as only He can into the hearts of human beings.

An old story from the Desert Fathers speaks to this elusive favor of the Holy Spirit. While His favor rests on the *obviously* saintly, it still "blows where it wishes, and you hear the sound of it, but cannot tell where it comes from and where it goes" (John 3:8):

Once when Abba Macarius was praying in his cell, he heard a voice that said, "Macarius, you have not yet reached the standard of two women in the city." On his arrival in the city, he found the house and knocked at the door. A woman opened it, and welcomed him to her house. He sat down, and called them to sit down with him.

Then he said to them, "It is for you that I have taken this long journey. Tell me how you live a religious life." They said, "Indeed, how can we lead a religious life? We were with our husbands last night." But the old man persuaded them to tell him their way of life.

Then they said, "We are both foreigners, in the world's eyes. But we accepted in marriage two brothers. Today we have been sharing this house for fifteen years. We do not know whether we have quarreled or said rude words to each other; but the whole of this time we have lived peaceably together. We thought we would enter a convent, and asked our husbands for permission, but they refused it. So since we could not get this permission, we have made a covenant between ourselves and God that a worldly word shall not pass our lips during the rest of our lives."

When Macarius heard this, he said, "Truly, it is not whether you are a virgin or a married woman, a monk or a man in the world: God gives His Holy Spirit to everyone, according to their earnestness of purpose."[50]

The Holy Spirit, "who art everywhere present and fillest all things," is also, as Saint Macarius learned, sent to "everyone, according to their earnestness of purpose." Sincerity in the search for God matters, yet we see in this story that the faith and behavior toward which that sincerity is channeled matter too.

The Jewish scribe who approached Jesus was *not far* from the kingdom of God. But *not far* does not mean *near enough*. The Orthodox Church embraces the scandal of Christ's exclusivity, confessing that there is no truth or salvation or knowledge of God apart from Him who is "the way, the truth, and the life" and without whom no one comes to the Father (John 14:6). Christ is the *unique* revelation of God, and because Christ identifies Himself with the Church, Orthodoxy also embraces the scandal that the Church is the *unique* revelation of Christ (Acts 9:4). That is to say, truth is definable: a particular God came to earth as a particular Man to preach a particular Kingdom and establish a particular Church in which alone is found a particular Salvation. An impenetrable mystery, however, is who is and who is not, from God's point of view, truly part of that Church. With Saint Paul, we "judge nothing before the time, until the Lord comes" (1 Cor. 4:5).

Truth is definable, identifiable, accessible, but it is also a treasure pursued by some persons who don't look or talk or think or live in ways familiar to us. The seventeenth chapter of the book of Acts describes a moment when the apostle Paul strolls through the Areopagus, a high hill in Athens on which was built a center of philosophical debate, and notices an altar built by pagans. They are religious people, he observes, and one of their altars bears the inscription TO THE UNKNOWN GOD. Saint Paul uses their altar as a point of commonality between his faith and their desire—like the Jewish scribe who approached Christ, these pagan Greeks were not far from the kingdom of God.

"The One whom you worship without knowing," he begins, "Him I proclaim to you." The apostle then describes a Lord of heaven and earth who has created everything and every nation, who cannot be contained within temples yet who has placed within humanity a yearning, "that they might grope for Him and find Him, though He is not far from each one of us; for in Him we live and move and have our being, as also some of your own poets have said, 'For we are also His offspring' " (Acts 17:22–28). Saint Paul affirms not only their yearning for God but also the seeds of truth as articulated by their own poets of pagan history.[51]

Much of Christian mission—then and now—involves nurturing nascent belief toward completion in Christ. "Though not with the same power as in the people of God [the Hebrews], nevertheless the presence of the Spirit of God also acted in the pagans who did not know the true God, because even among them God found for Himself chosen people," wrote Saint Herman of Alaska, among the first, in the eighteenth century, to bring Orthodox Christianity to the shores of America.

Such, for instance, were the virgin prophetesses called Sibyls who vowed virginity to an unknown God, but still to God the Creator of the universe, the all-powerful ruler of the world, as He was conceived by the pagans. Though the pagan philosophers also wandered in the darkness of ignorance of God, yet they sought the Truth which is beloved by God; and on account of this God-pleasing seeking, they could partake of the Spirit of God, for it is said that the nations who do not know God practice by nature the demands of the law and do what is pleasing to God [cf. Rom. 2:14].

So you see, both in the holy Hebrew people, a people beloved by God, and in the pagans who did not know God, there was preserved a knowledge of God—that is, a clear

and rational comprehension of how our Lord God the Holy
Spirit acts in man, and by means of what inner and outer
feelings one can be sure that this is really the action of our
Lord God the Holy Spirit and not a delusion of the enemy.
That is how it was from Adam's fall until the coming in the
flesh of our Lord Jesus Christ into the world.[52]

The Holy Spirit is immanent and the Holy Spirit is
transcendent; He is "everywhere present and fillest all things,"
and He is wholly other and above all being; His truth is precise
and knowable, and His truth is above all categories of precision
and knowing; He is ours alone, and He is everyone's equally.
The ways He moves cannot be counted, but they all lead to the
same place: to a sense of wonder in the living God.

The troubled man who had received the comfort of the Holy
Spirit through the gentle knock on the head from Elder Paisios
recalls a time when he was driving the saintly monk somewhere
in his car. "Elder," the man said, "tell me about God. What is He
like? Speak to me."

The elder didn't say a word, so I simply continued to
drive up the curving mountain road in silence. Suddenly, I
began to feel God's presence everywhere: in the car, out in
the hills, and to the reaches of the farthest galaxies. He was
"everywhere present and filling all things," without being
identified with any of them. He permeated everything,
without being mixed or confused with anything. Being

Spirit, the ever-existent God permeated the material cosmos, without ever being identified with changeable matter. Being Spirit, God dwelt in the eternity of an infinite present, containing past, present, and future.[53]

5
Treasury of Good Things

O heavenly King, the Comforter, the Spirit of truth, Who art
everywhere present and fillest all things; Treasury of good
things and Giver of life; come and abide in us, and cleanse
us from every impurity, and save our souls, O Gracious Lord.

•

*I*n the Holy Spirit is the fountain of divine
treasures; for from Him cometh wisdom, awe,
and understanding. To Him, therefore, be praise,
glory, might, and honor."[54] The Orthodox
Church has embedded her theology in song and liturgy, so
the simple act of going to church is a big part of how faith
and commitment are passed from generation to generation.
This brief hymn to the Holy Spirit from the morning service
of Matins reminds us that our blessings ultimately come from
outside ourselves—a good lesson for any generation to learn.
The "divine treasures" we enjoy are not ours by nature but by
the grace of the Holy Spirit.

The most valuable of those treasures were considered in
chapter 3—the truths that the Holy Spirit reveals about
the Holy Trinity, about ourselves, and about the Church.
To these treasures that define the Christian faith are added
treasures that adorn the Christian person. These include the

beautiful attributes described by the apostle Paul in Galatians 5:22–23:

> The fruit of the Spirit is love, joy, peace, patience, kindness, goodness, faithfulness, gentleness, self-control.

These nine jewels beautify whoever possesses them. Properly understood, however, they beautify whoever possesses *Him*. Christian life consists not in reaching for the fruit but in acquiring the Spirit.

There is a difference between fruit and Tree, between treasure and King, between gift and Giver. The Christian receives the one but pursues the other. The prodigal son, in Luke 15, returns to the loving embrace of his father and not to the loving embrace of the nice robe or the shiny rings or the new sandals or the fatted calf—all of which are given to him upon his return. His fundamental relationship is not with the good things, but with his father, from whom all those good things flow.

Bookending the nine attributes of the Spirit in Galatians 5 are calls to "walk in the Spirit" (verses 16 and 25). This suggests that we are not to fixate on the individual fruit, as if the nine attributes were nine strategies for becoming a better person— adding one fruit to become more loving, one to become more joyful, one to become more peaceful. The call here is not to *walk in the fruit* but to *walk in the Spirit*.

Consider, for example, the counsel of Saint Seraphim of Sarov, a beloved Russian monk of the early nineteenth century: "Acquire the Spirit of peace, and a thousand souls around you will be saved."[55] At first pass, we might hear Saint Seraphim saying: be more peaceful; become a peaceful person; go and do peaceful things. Armed with what we believe to be his advice, we might fill our time with charitable projects and good deeds and breathing exercises. Notice, however, that Saint Seraphim did not say to us to acquire *peace*. Instead, he directs us to acquire *the Spirit*.

Is the distinction important? The prayer to the Holy Spirit refers to Him as the "Treasury of good things," so to reach for the fruit of Galatians 5 instead of reaching for the Spirit is to grasp for the good things without having acquired the Good Treasury. It's like trying to live like God apart from God. The goal of Christian life is not to force our behavior to fit categories of "love," "joy," "peace," and the rest—if that were true, Christian experience would merely be an external gloss, like adding a fresh coat of paint to a house that really needs a new foundation. We would be working on the wrong problem.

We all recognize the futility of trying to improve behavior without taming the heart. The Christian may go to church and sing hymns and give alms and adorn the world with plentiful evidence of faith yet still fly into a rage when provoked or seethe with jealousy when slighted or burn with lust when aroused or swell with pride when praised. So some deeper change is needed.

Christian life is about becoming a *new creation* in Christ; it's the daily renewal of the *inward man* (2 Cor. 5:17 and 4:16). It is to follow Saint Seraphim's advice to acquire not peace in and of itself, but the Spirit of peace. Such inner renewal brings the heart under the control of the Holy Spirit, who then releases the attributes of Galatians 5 *through us* according to His time,

His measure, His purpose, and His glory. If severed from their source, these nine treasures of the "Treasury of good things"—love, joy, peace, patience, kindness, goodness, faithfulness, gentleness, self-control—become tarnished. They lose proper expression and become vulnerable to our clever, even dark, designs.

Without the Holy Spirit, *love* degenerates into lust or sentimentality or mere companionship. We reach for another out of selfishness or insecurity or loneliness; we become motivated by deep needs that ignore boundaries. We crave intense feelings, even drama, and instead of pursuing something noble we settle for the emotionalism that true love is not. With the Holy Spirit, love makes both the giver and the receiver well, even holy. We suffer long and kindly. We do not envy or parade ourselves or act puffed up; rather, we rejoice in the truth and bear all things, believe all things, hope all things, and endure all things (1 Cor. 13:4–7). Relationships are born and grow in freedom. "Where the Spirit of the Lord is," Saint Paul wrote, "there is liberty" (2 Cor. 3:17). To acquire the Holy Spirit is to become the love that is divine, healing, free.

Without the Holy Spirit, *joy* degenerates into the pursuit of pleasure. We maneuver through life solely to avoid pain. We pursue only light and lose the ability to embrace the darkness so necessary for spiritual growth. We imperceptibly knit ourselves to the fabric of this passing world with its transitory comforts. Because we live in search of the next good time, we grow weak. With the Holy Spirit, joy is not forced to become happiness. We are willing to sacrifice pleasure and happiness so that joy, which is not as dependent on circumstance, might emerge. We rest in the promises of God that run deeper than everything that troubles life's surface. We know how to rejoice with those who rejoice, seeking nothing of our own and feeling no competition. To acquire the Holy Spirit is to embrace joy and reject its counterfeits.

Without the Holy Spirit, *peace* degenerates into an avoidance of all conflict, some of which is vital to healthy relationships. We seek exterior tranquility as a distraction from inner turmoil. We lose principles worth defending and differences worth celebrating. We underestimate humanity's capacity for evil, most especially our own. With the Holy Spirit, peace reserves the right to a special kind of violence—the kind required to seize the kingdom of God (Matt. 11:12). We wage war with no one's old nature but our own; we calmly battle passions that refuse to die easily. We discover an inner stillness. We do not react and we do not resent. We grow undisturbed by troubling thoughts as the heart enters a state of quiet listening. Because we have accepted this daily and quiet martyrdom, we grow into vessels of stillness that benefit others. To acquire the Holy Spirit is to become the peace that passes understanding (Phil. 4:7).

Without the Holy Spirit, *patience* degenerates into sloth. We lose the ability to do what needs to be done when it needs to be done. We grow tolerant of inappropriate delay; we lose the relationship between justice and timing. We mistake laziness for perseverance. We neglect. With the Holy Spirit, patience pursues, but does not rush, a desired outcome. We do not force an agenda; we resist our need for control. We exercise the right restraint at the right time in the right way. We understand that no one can disturb our interior peace without our permission.

We trust in God's timing and in His way of doing things. We accept that true soul work is often slow, unhurried, mundane. To acquire the Holy Spirit is to discern the difference between waiting and hesitating.

Without the Holy Spirit, *kindness* degenerates into a lack of resolve. We lose the ability to say no. We erode the boundaries that define our personhood. We pacify beyond what is healthy, even enabling another's self-destruction. We draw near when distance is called for and remain distant when nearness is needed. We forget what anger is for. With the Holy Spirit, kindness is not defeated by fatigue or prejudice or argument. We learn when an acquaintance should remain an acquaintance, and when an acquaintance should become a friend. We become generous and are not devastated when there is no return. We are honest, but not cruel; warm, but not seductive. To acquire the Holy Spirit is to express kindness while a storm of irritability may rage within.

Without the Holy Spirit, *goodness* degenerates into mere morality. We focus on external behavior and forget the condition of the heart. We compare ourselves with others, and usually come out favorably. We grow smug. We become legalistic, shallow, bland. With the Holy Spirit, goodness becomes empathy. We grow sensitive to those in need, including ourselves. Being right becomes less important than becoming righteous. Our understanding of the good transcends contemporary trends and cultural taste. We learn where true good is from and where it leads; we discern the fingerprints of God. To acquire the Holy Spirit is to discern God in all good and all good in God.

Without the Holy Spirit, *faithfulness* degenerates into inertia. We favor predictability over risk; we get stuck. We mistake fear for perseverance. We lose identity, energy, and those qualities that distinguish us. We waste time, accomplish nothing, and fail to make the world a better place because we were here. We lack vision. With the Holy Spirit, faithfulness means we become not stuck but still. Distractions do not reach a heart that abides in a state of constant listening, so that when God says to move, we move. We follow where He leads, willing even to enter the dark. We are obedient but free; we voluntarily suffer. We choose the way of God even when no one is watching. To acquire the Holy Spirit is to understand faith as inseparable from faithfulness.

Without the Holy Spirit, *gentleness* degenerates into a lack of boundaries. We lose willpower; we become passive. Assertiveness looks too much like aggression, and decisiveness too much like violence. Men, in fear, swerve toward the safe, the joyless, the weak; women favor the shy, the sentimental, the self-protective. With the Holy Spirit, gentleness becomes hospitality. We keep a reign on ourselves and make room for others to grow in our midst. We learn how to resist forcing ourselves on others, in body, will, and opinion. We use a light touch if it will put people at ease and a heavy touch when necessary, but with grace. Silence no longer disturbs but nourishes. To acquire the Holy Spirit is to harness the powerful energy of meekness.

Without the Holy Spirit, *self-control* degenerates into self-suffocation. We lose vibrancy; we lose life's vivifying energy. We grow rigid and legalistic and recoil from what appears uncontrollable. The proper goals of discipline are lost as discipline becomes the goal itself. We intimidate others and provoke their suspicion. With the Holy Spirit, self-control means we become God's clean instrument. We embrace fasting, prayer, and understand the role of the body in acquiring or losing salvation. Moderation is seen as strength and not weakness. Because we neither indulge the self nor obsess over the self, we can restrain or celebrate as an occasion calls for. With the Holy Spirit, willpower is delivered from the tyranny of the flesh.

The prayer to the Holy Spirit calls this "Treasury of good things" to "come and abide in us." We do not approach God as a cosmic slot machine, feeding Him with the right formula of prayers and good deeds for the purpose of gaining a jackpot of favors in return. Instead, we are like children, who, as we grow and mature, discover that our true relationship all along was not with the gifts given to us by our Caretaker but with the Caretaker Himself. To keep that relationship alive, God may grant His gifts to us in measure and withdraw them for a season. "Why did the tongues appear to be divided among [the disciples]?" asks Saint Gregory Palamas. "Because the Spirit is given by measure by the Father to all except Christ. . . . Each one obtained different gifts, lest anyone should suppose the grace given to the saints by the Holy Spirit was theirs by nature."[56]

And when grace falls upon the ready soul, the chest of treasures overflows. Nine becomes no longer a number but a symbol of the numberless gifts that pour from the Holy Spirit. Saint Seraphim of Sarov gave us the counsel to "acquire the Spirit of peace," but he also gave us a radiant example of what acquiring the Spirit can mean. Material treasures shine, but, as his experience of the Holy Spirit reveals, not as brightly as the person who fully acquires the immaterial "Treasury of good things," an acquisition that begins, according to Saint Seraphim, in the cleansing waters of baptism.

Nicholas Motovilov had been a friend of Saint Seraphim's and a beneficiary, literally, of the saint's spiritual treasures. He tells this story about a moment in a forest glade with the humble Russian *staretz*—or saintly elder—and a most unexpected event:

It was Thursday; it was a grey day and the ground was covered with a thick layer of snow. Great flakes were still falling when Father Seraphim began talking to me in the glade close by his Near Hermitage, on the banks of the Sorovka. He seated me on a recently-felled tree-trunk and sat down opposite to me.

"The Lord has shown me," he said, "that when you were a child you wanted to know the goal of the Christian life and that you had put this question to a number of eminent ecclesiastics." I must confess that this question had indeed weighed heavily on my mind since I was twelve, and that I had often asked it without receiving a satisfactory reply.

"Yet no one," continued Father Seraphim, "told you anything definite. They instructed you to go to church, to pray, to do good works, telling you that there lay the goal of the Christian life. Some of them even said to you: 'Don't search into things that are beyond you.' Well, miserable servant of God that I am, I am going to try to explain to you what this goal is.

"Prayer, fasting, works of mercy—all this is very good, but it represents only the means, not the end of the Christian life. The true end is the acquisition of the Holy Spirit."

"What do you mean by acquisition," I asked the father, "I don't quite understand."

"To acquire means to gain possession," he replied. "You know what it means to earn money, don't you? Well, it is the same with the Holy Spirit. The aim of some men is to grow rich, to receive honors and distinctions. The Holy Spirit himself is also capital, but eternal capital. Our Lord compares our life to trading and the works of this life to buying: 'Buy from me gold . . . that you me be rich' (Rev. 3.18). 'Make the most of the time, because the days are evil' (Eph. 5.16). The only valuables on earth are good works done for Christ: these win us the grace of the Holy Spirit. No good works can bring us the fruits of the Holy Spirit unless they are done for love of Christ. That is why the Lord himself said, 'He who does not gather with me, scatters.'

"For the essential thing is not just to do good but to acquire the Holy Spirit as the one eternal treasure which will never pass away. The grace of the Holy Spirit, given at baptism in the name of the Father, and of the Son, and of the Holy Spirit, continues to shine in our heart as divine light in spite of our falls and the darkness of our soul. It is this grace that cries in us to the Father: 'Abba, Father!' "

"But how," I asked him, "can I know that I am within this grace of the Holy Spirit. How I long to understand completely."

Then Father Seraphim gripped me firmly by the shoulders and said: "My friend, both of us, at this moment, are in the Holy Spirit, you and I. Why won't you look at me?"

"I can't look at you, Father, because the light flashing from your eyes and face is brighter than the sun and I'm dazzled!"

"Don't be afraid, friend of God, you yourself are shining just like I am; you too are now in the fullness of the grace of the Holy Spirit, otherwise you wouldn't be able to see me as you do."

And, leaning toward me, Father Seraphim said quietly: "Thank the Lord for his ineffable goodness: you may have noticed that I didn't even make the sign of the cross; only in my heart I said this prayer to the Lord: 'Lord, grant him the grace of seeing clearly, with the eyes of the flesh, that outpouring of your Spirit which you vouchsafe to your servants when you condescend to reveal yourself to them in the reflection of your glory.' "

Then I looked at the Staretz and was panic-stricken. Picture, in the sun's orb, in the most dazzling brightness of the noon-day shining, the face of a man who is talking to you. You see his lips moving, the expression in his eyes, you hear his voice, you feel his arms round your shoulders, and yet you see neither his arms, nor his body, nor his face, you lose all sense of yourself, you can see only the blinding light which spreads everywhere, lighting up the layer of snow covering the glade, and igniting the flakes that are falling on us both like white powder.

"What do you feel?" asked Father Seraphim.

"An amazing well-being!" I replied.

"But what exactly is it?"

"I feel a great calm in my soul, a peace which no words can express."

"This is the peace, friend of God, which the Lord promised to his disciples when he said: 'Peace I leave with you, my peace I give to you; not as the world gives do I give to you' (John 14.27). It is that peace which the Apostle calls 'the peace which passes all under-standing' (Phil. 4.7). This is what is filling your heart now. And what else do you feel?"

"An amazing happiness fills my heart."

Father Seraphim went on: "When the Holy Spirit descends and fills the soul with the plenitude of his presence, then we experience that joy which Christ described, the joy which the world cannot take away. However, the joy you now feel in your heart is nothing compared to that which Paul the Apostle describes: 'What no eye has seen, nor ear has heard, nor the heart of man conceived, what God has prepared for those who love him' (I Cor. 2.9). The first fruits of that joy are already given us and if our soul is even now filled with such glad sweetness, what words can express the joy laid up in heaven for those who sorrow here below? And you too, friend of God, have had grief in your life; see how joyfully God has already comforted you in this world. Do you feel anything else, my friend?'

"I'm amazingly warm."

"Warm? What are you saying, my friend? We are in the depths of the forest, in mid-winter, the snow lies under our feet and is settling on our clothes. How can you be warm?"

"It's the warmth one feels in a hot bath."

"Does it smell like that?"

"Oh no, nothing on earth can be compared to this! There's no scent in all the world like this one!"

"I know," said Father Seraphim, smiling, "It's the same with me. I'm only questioning you to find out what you're discovering. It is indeed true, friend of God, that no scent on earth can be compared with this fragrance, because it comes from the Holy Spirit. By the way, you've just told me that you've been feeling the warmth of a hot bath, but look: the snow settling on us isn't melting, neither on you nor on me. That shows that the warmth isn't in the air but is within us. This is what the Holy Spirit causes us to ask God for when we cry to him: 'Kindle in us the fire of the Holy Spirit!' This is as it should be, for divine grace comes to live in our hearts, within us. This kingdom is just the grace of the Holy Spirit, living in us, warming us, enlightening us, filling the air with his scent, delighting us with his fragrance and rejoicing our hearts with an ineffable gladness. At this moment we are with those whom the Lord mentions as not tasting death before they see the kingdom of God come with power (Luke 9.27; Mark 9.1).

"Now you know, my friend, what it's like to be in the fullness of the Holy Spirit. This is what we are filled with today, in spite of our unworthiness. Treasure this memory of the revelation given you of the fathomless loving-kindness of God who has visited you today."[57]

6
Giver of Life

O heavenly King, the Comforter, the Spirit of truth, Who art
everywhere present and fillest all things; Treasury of good
things and Giver of life; come and abide in us, and cleanse
us from every impurity, and save our souls, O Gracious Lord.

•

*I*n one icon of the radiant transfiguration of
Saint Seraphim of Sarov in the forest, the light
of the grace of the Holy Spirit shining through
him spills onto the leaves and grass and bushes
nearby. It's a moment when biological life meets spiritual life, and
it's not just a technique for an icon but a principle proclaimed
by Orthodox Christians with greenery of our own during the
liturgical season of Pentecost.

Christians around the world harvest and bring verdant life
into the churches for Pentecost. Why greenery? Not because of
the life that ferns and flowers have but because of the life toward
which they point. Pentecost is a particular kind of celebration,
for it celebrates a particular kind of life—the Holy Spirit, the
"Giver of life," as the prayer calls Him, descends upon the
Church and gives Himself.

Consider biological life. There is often a sweetness surrounding the news of a pregnancy or a birth, for it arouses within us both new love and soothing assurance that life will go on. But in the shadow of that sweetness—understandably overlooked—lies tragedy. "Corruption," wrote Saint Gregory of Nyssa, referring to death's long and terrible reach, "has its beginning from birth."[58] Embedded in every birth is mortality; a person born is a person who will die. Smiles on one end of life give way to cries on the other.

While there are some who believe that death is a phenomenon of God—that He created it and wields it for punishment—Orthodox Christianity understands death to be not the creation of God but the sad contribution of humanity. The natural state of Adam was union with God, the Source of life, so with the fall of Adam came the rupture of his natural state and the break from his connection with life. Properly speaking, no one ever dies of *natural causes*, because the nature that God created has no death in it. Instead, death is humanity's dark paint splattered on the pristine canvas of God's creation. Death was the consequence of the unnatural act of sin in Eden and the consequence inherited by every man, woman, and child since. Death is the natural consequence of an unnatural condition.

It is death, and not the guilt of sin, that the rest of humanity has inherited from the fall of Adam and Eve. Early Church Fathers did not understand the fall of our first parents to have passed on a kind of "guilt by association" to subsequent generations. Adam and Eve were solely responsible for their own sins. Death, however, spread to us all.

One fifth-century bishop, Saint Cyril of Alexandria, explains it this way:

> Yes, Adam indeed fell and, having ignored the divine commandment, was condemned to corruptibility and death. But how did many become sinners because of him? What are his missteps to us? How could all of us who were not yet born be condemned together with him. . . . In Adam, human nature fell ill and became subject to corruptibility through disobedience, and, therefore the passions entered in.[59]

Death is the monstrous cave that obscures eternity. We who are bound by time and space cannot see past this great obstacle, and we are unsure what precisely awaits us when we enter it. Those who believe the Bible know that biological life alone, as precious as it is, does not qualify a person for safe passage. Instead, something more is needed.

That *something more* is what the greenery of Pentecost is intended to suggest: the life of mere biology meets the life of pure Spirit. Recall the story of Christ and Nicodemus conversing under the cover of night: "Rabbi," said Nicodemus, "we know that You are a teacher come from God; for no one can do these signs that You do unless God is with him." Here, Christ identifies the limitations of biological life and points to the need for something greater: "Most assuredly, I say to you, unless one is born again, he cannot see the kingdom of God" (John 3:2–3).

We may understand born *again* to mean born *from above*, or even *from the top*. A new birth is necessary, a new start—a transformation

rooted in something beyond ourselves that enables us to transform the tragedy of death into a final and ultimate victory of
life. The Lord further describes the new birth: "Unless one is
born of water and the Spirit, he cannot enter the kingdom of
God. That which is born of the flesh is flesh, and that which is
born of the Spirit is spirit" (John 3:5–6).

That is to say, truth is definable: a particular God came to earth
as a particular Man to preach a particular Kingdom and establish a
particular Church in which alone is found a particular Salvation.

From its earliest days, the Christian Church has recognized
this "water" as the water of baptism and this "Spirit" as the grace
of the Holy Spirit. *Water* and *Spirit* form a single cleansing motion
from above, just as God, through the prophecy of Ezekiel, said
it would: "I shall sprinkle clean water on you, and you will be
cleansed from all your uncleanness, and I will also cleanse you
from all your idols. I shall give you a new heart and put a new
spirit within you. I shall take the heart of stone from your flesh
and give you a heart of flesh. I shall put My Spirit within you"
(Ezek. 36:25–27).

The baptism of Christ in the Jordan River, though He had
no fallen nature from which to be cleansed, and the descent of
the Holy Spirit upon Him in the form of a dove forever fixed in
the mind of the Church the necessity of baptism for those who
desire to transcend death. Just as biological life begins in the
water of the womb, eternal life begins in the water of the font.
As early Christians understood, the font becomes both a *tomb*
for the old nature and a *womb* for the new; the water of baptism
becomes, as Saint Cyril, the fourth-century bishop of Jerusalem,
noted, "at once your grave and your mother."[60]

In Orthodox baptism, water and Spirit come together in a single grace-filled experience, or *sacrament*. A sacrament is neither magic nor mere ceremony; it's a deep integration of the physical world with the spiritual world, both of which are part of the whole Kingdom of God, and it's how a human being begins and sustains a lifelong connection with the living God. "In most of the sacraments," writes the contemporary Orthodox bishop Kallistos Ware, "the Church takes material things—water, bread, wine, oil—and makes them a vehicle of the Spirit. In this way the sacraments look back to the Incarnation, when Christ took material flesh and made it a vehicle of the Spirit."[61] God deals with our total reality—matter, body, soul, mind, spirit—saving and glorifying it all, and doing it all together. The Creator embraces the whole of His seen and unseen creation.

Just as love is a difficult concept to appreciate apart from the concrete expressions of it, the Holy Spirit is difficult to comprehend apart from His specific actions within creation. Sacraments help with this. We may better understand what a sacrament is by considering what a sacrament accomplishes.

Imagine, for example, you've just purchased a brand new appliance. It's been delivered to your house and you have the perfect place for it. You remove the appliance from the box and recycle all the packaging. You pore through the owner's manual to discover all the helpful things your new appliance can do. You've educated yourself on its features; it's shiny, powerful, and ready to perform.

Now, imagine that you never plug your new appliance in to the wall socket. Suddenly, what purpose does it serve? None. What can it do? Nothing. What features does it have? Doesn't matter. Instead of a fully functioning item operating to the best of its ability, this appliance merely takes up space without doing what it was created to do. Why? Because it has no connection with electricity—the source of its effectiveness.

From the earliest days of our faith, Christians have always understood ourselves to be something like appliances. Authentic Christian life—as established by Jesus Christ, practiced by His disciples, and passed on by faithful men and women through the ages—is not possible unless we are plugged into the Source. We can walk through life adorned with gifts and talents and great potential, but unless we are connected to the God who created us and knows exactly what we can do, we simply take up space and will never become what we were created to become. "His divine power," writes the apostle Peter in his second epistle, "has given to us all things that pertain to life and godliness" (2 Pet. 1:3).

This connectivity does not happen automatically, no more than the plug of an appliance finds its own way to a wall socket. So Christian life has always consisted of two parts, organically united and working together to change a person from within.

The first part may be called *imitation*. Imitation is the name given to how we are called to live day by day. The Christian is an imitator of Jesus Christ. We go through our days imitating the Christ of the Gospels—we do and say and think on things Christianly. We pray, serve others, invest in people, tell the truth, enjoy life, fast, create and love creation, and strive to be compassionate. The treasures that we have received from the "Treasury of good things" we use to be good to others. "Be imitators of God," wrote Saint Paul, "and walk in love" (Eph.

5:1–2). Imitation of Christ is absolutely necessary, and one cannot call oneself Christian if one is not imitating Christ. But imitation is only one part of Christian life. Indeed, imitation *alone* can mean we become merely actors who read someone else's lines and take on another's mannerisms without experiencing any personal inward transformation. Imitation, then, needs the second part of Christian life.

This part may be called *participation*. If imitation is the external act, participation is the internal reality. Participation is actually plugging into the Source. For Orthodox Christians, this means something very specific: the sacramental life of the Church.

Here the human being embraces and transcends biological life and communes with the divine life of the Holy Trinity. The sacraments are those moments when we literally plug into the Holy Spirit, who then enables us to participate in the very life of Christ. Or, in the case of baptism, into the very death of Christ: "As many of us as were baptized into Christ Jesus were baptized into His death" (Rom. 6:3).

The sacramental life enables us to embrace our own natural boundaries and, in actual fact, enter through them mystically into the reality of the living God. In the power of the Holy Spirit, present in every sacrament, the Christian exchanges his or her mortal life for Christ's immortal life. "The Word of God assumed humanity," wrote Saint Athanasius, the fourth-century bishop of Alexandria, "that we might become God."[62] That is, that we might undergo what ancient Christians called *deification*—becoming by grace all that God is by nature: a human being becomes not the nature, or essence, of God, but rather becomes immortal, everlasting, subject to no death or decay.

Imitation is to *behave as Christ did*; participation is to *become who Christ is*, or more precisely, to take His everlasting life within us—it is the real and intimate connection with God that cannot happen through mere imitation alone. It's important, however, not to press the categorizations too far—prayer, for example, can be both imitation and participation. The categories exist not to rigidly define the salvation experience but to aid us in approaching wonders that ultimately lie beyond our comprehension.

The Orthodox Church informally recognizes seven sacraments as having particular significance. These must not be understood as isolated acts accomplishing unrelated purposes, but as integrated elements of one whole life in God. And we say informally, because Orthodoxy has never rigidly fixed the number of sacraments at seven; indeed, the number has varied through the centuries. These seven, in the order in which they may be experienced, make most modern lists: baptism, chrismation, Holy Communion, confession, marriage, ordination to holy orders, anointing of the sick. When approached in the fear of God, with faith and love, these sacraments, or *mysteries*, are primary experiences of participation—they nurture within those who partake of them a sacramental worldview that, over time, sees the whole creation as a sacrament, alive with the vivifying presence of God. That is to say, they impart to those who partake of them the Holy Spirit, the "Giver of life."

In the sacrament of baptism, the Giver of life begins the giving of Himself. Standing over the baptismal font before immersing the *catechumen*—or, one who has been under instruction—the priest calls down the grace of the Holy Spirit upon the water:

That this water may be sanctified with the power, and effectual operation, and indwelling of the Holy Spirit. . . . That there may be sent down into it the grace of redemption, the blessing of Jordan. . . . That there may come upon this water the purifying operation of the super-substantial Trinity.

When the Holy Spirit descends upon the font, the water within becomes much more than two parts hydrogen, one part oxygen. In a sense, the water becomes one full part material and one full part spiritual; it remains completely water, yet is mystically filled with grace and able to impart divine life. Then, moments before an *old humanity* enters the water and a *new humanity* emerges from it, the priest makes the sign of the cross over the water three times and prays:

But do Thou, Master of all, show this water to be the water of redemption, the water of sanctification, the purification of flesh and spirit, the loosing of bonds, the remission of sins, the illumination of the soul, the vessel of regeneration, the renewal of the spirit, the gift of adoption to sonship, the garment of incorruption, the fountain of life.

The adult, youth, or infant readied for reception into the Orthodox Church is immersed three times by the priest into the baptismal waters, accomplishing the death of the old fallen nature and the birth of the new purified one. The Giver of life has given Himself to the receptive soul in the sacrament of baptism. For the newly washed, the task now will be to preserve this baptismal grace alive and growing through a life of sustained repentance.

The transformation of a person in baptism begins in what one fifth-century monk called "the innermost and uncontaminated chamber of the heart,"[63] beneath the circuitry of conscious feeling. In the wake of the baptism itself, with skin still soft and hair still wet, one feels exhilaration. This rush subsides with time as the newly baptized settles into a simpler mode of gradually heightening perception. He begins the journey of living with God's own heart.

This growth in sensitivity toward the things of God, rooted in a life of personal repentance and supernatural grace, leads a person toward a new encounter with the water and the Spirit of baptism—the *gift of tears*. This "water from the Spirit" flows from the baptismal experience and it, too, transforms. The gift of tears cleanses, purifies, refines; and because cleansing, purification, and refinement are foundational to a life worthy of heaven, the water of the tears given by the Holy Spirit may be included in Christ's words to Nicodemus, that "unless one is born of water and the Spirit, he cannot enter the kingdom of God" (John 3:5).

The gift of tears reveals that the transformation begun in the sacrament of baptism has been working its way through a person, like the smoke of incense rising through a temple, transforming the deep self into a pliable and perceptive instrument of God. It is indeed a gift and not something forced or manufactured. These tears are not an emotional or psychological phenomenon but pass through the emotions and the psyche without being rooted in either.

For Saint John Climacus, whose *Ladder of Divine Ascent* is read aloud in many monasteries each year during Lent, the gift of tears given by the Holy Spirit is a natural continuation of the cleansing begun in the sacrament of baptism. That is to say, the Giver of life gives life, and that life includes continual repentance and blessed mourning. It is, however, a mourning of joy and not despair. In step seven of the *Ladder*, Saint John writes:

> Greater than baptism itself is the fountain of tears after baptism, even though it is somewhat audacious to say so. For baptism is the washing away of evils that were in us before, but sins committed after baptism are washed away by tears. As baptism is received in infancy, we have all defiled it, but we cleanse it anew with tears. And if God in His love for mankind had not given us tears, those being saved would be few indeed and hard to find.[64]

For most of us, death sends postcards long before we draw our last bodily breath, in the form of illness or sorrow or disappointment. Each of these, because they bring to life a dark or depressing tone, is a form of death—a kind of dusk before the real dark.

So, we yearn for something more. While biological life needs just a moment of urge and opportunity, spiritual rebirth requires a power beyond our capacity to produce. It requires a power holy enough to change into good whatever it touches. "Verily, the Holy Spirit doth overflow with streams and passages of grace and doth water all creation with invigorating life."[65] The

Giver of life gives Himself. This is the life that death cannot hold. This is liberation.

The feast of Pentecost, with its shower of green foliage in the churches, is a celebration of this liberation. The palms that adorn the icons and the pines that adorn the walls are like arrows that point our attention toward greater realities. Because He is the Spirit of God, the life He imparts is always new, always eternal, always immortal. In the famous icon of the Holy Trinity by Andrei Rublev and often used at Pentecost, the figure symbolizing the Holy Spirit is adorned in a green robe.

"All things thirsting for holiness turn to Him," wrote Saint Basil the Great in *On the Holy Spirit*, "and everything living in virtue never turns away from Him." He continues:

> He waters them with His life-giving breath and helps them reach their proper fulfillment. He perfects all other things, and Himself lacks nothing; He gives life to all things, and is never depleted. He does not increase by additions, but is always complete, self-established, and present everywhere. He is the source of sanctification, spiritual light, who gives illumination to everyone using His powers to search for the truth—and the illumination He gives is Himself.[66]

7
Come and Abide in Us

O heavenly King, the Comforter, the Spirit of truth, Who art
everywhere present and fillest all things; Treasury of good
things and Giver of life; come and abide in us, and cleanse
us from every impurity, and save our souls, O Gracious Lord.

•

To attend an Orthodox Christian baptism
is to observe more than a body and a few
towels getting wet. The service of baptism
does not end when a person emerges
from the baptismal font, dries off, and grabs a plate of food
at an after-party. Rather, between the action in the font and
the reception in the fellowship hall, another sacrament unfolds
that involves the Holy Spirit in a special way. So, let's visit an
Orthodox baptism to discover what happens next.

An adult woman we will call Catherine has just been baptized.
There she stands, clothed in a white robe and a wide smile.
Friends and family are in attendance, and there's a good turnout
from her new congregation. So far, Catherine has been prayed
over; exorcized; has renounced and spat upon Satan; has recited
the Nicene Creed as the summary of what she believes; has
been anointed with oil; and has been immersed three times in

a baptismal font in street clothing that, since it symbolizes her former way of life, she will never wear again. Not a bad way to spend thirty minutes.

But the service is not over. Baptism alone is not enough for Catherine, just as it was not enough for the newly baptized believers in Samaria after the apostle Philip preached Christ to them (Acts 8:4–17). When the old orientation of the fallen nature has been removed from a person's life through baptism, a new orientation must take its place. The Spirit must replace the flesh as the guiding force in life.

To understand this new orientation, we may recall an image Jesus used: "When an unclean spirit goes out of a man, he goes through dry places, seeking rest, and finds none. Then he says, 'I will return to my house from which I came.' And when he comes, he finds it empty, swept and put in order. Then he goes and takes with him seven other spirits more wicked than himself, and they enter and dwell there; and the last state of that man is worse than the first" (Matt. 12:43–45).

While Catherine's physical and spiritual house has been swept clean in the sacrament of baptism, it must now be filled so that it's no longer empty and vulnerable. Tertullian, writing in the Christian community of the second century, describes what happens next: "When we have come out of the baptismal font, we are thoroughly anointed with a blessed oil. The oil runs over the body, but profits us spiritually."[67] This is the sacrament of *chrismation*—the anointing of the newly baptized with *chrism*, or special oil prepared only by a bishop, for the purpose of being sealed with the gift of the Holy Spirit. Chrismation is the first formal invitation to the Holy Spirit to, as the prayer to Him says, "come and abide in us."

Catherine's priest begins her chrismation by offering aloud this prayer:

Blessed art Thou, O Lord God Almighty, Source of all good things, Sun of righteousness, Who sheddest forth upon them who were in darkness the light of salvation, through the manifestation of Thine Only-begotten Son and our God; and Who hast given unto us, unworthy though we be, blessed purification through hallowed water, and divine sanctification, through life-giving chrismation; who now, also, hast been graciously pleased to regenerate Thy servant who hath newly received Illumination by water and the Spirit, and grantest unto her remission of sins, whether voluntary or involuntary. Do Thou, the same Master, compassionate King of all, grant also unto her the seal of the gift of Thy holy, and almighty, and adorable Spirit, and participation in the holy Body and the precious Blood of Thy Christ. Keep her in Thy sanctification; confirm her in the Orthodox faith; deliver her from the Evil One, and from the machinations of the same. And preserve her soul in purity and uprightness, through the saving fear of Thee; that she may please Thee in every deed and word, and may be a child and heir of Thy heavenly kingdom. For Thou art our God, the God who showeth mercy and saveth; and unto Thee do we ascribe glory: to the Father and to the Son and to the Holy Spirit: now and ever, and unto ages of ages. Amen.

Now the priest turns toward the newly baptized Catherine. With a crosslike motion of a small brush dipped in chrism, the priest anoints the doorways of her senses: her eyes, ears, nostrils, lips, hands, even her forehead, chest, back, and feet. This anointing imparts the power of the Holy Spirit over everything the newly baptized will experience in this world but also over everything the world will experience through this newly baptized. Both what a person invites into the self and expresses from the self must be redeemed.

Too, this anointing carries within it the possibility of sharp discernment of truth from falsehood—a deeply necessary gift in a world of shadow and deception. "These things I have written to you concerning those who try to deceive you," offers Saint John in his first epistle, "but the anointing which you have received from Him abides in you, and you do not need that anyone teach you; but as the same anointing teaches you concerning all things, and is true, and is not a lie, and just as it has taught you, you will abide in Him" (1 John 2:26–27).

With each application of the chrism, the priest announces, "The seal of the gift of the Holy Spirit." And the congregation, standing in a spirit of joy around the newly baptized, calls out in one voice for every part of that anointing, "Seal!" The priest announces, the faithful respond, but ultimately God does the work. "Now He who establishes us with you in Christ and has anointed us is God, who also has sealed us and given us the Spirit in our hearts as a guarantee" (2 Cor. 1:21–22).

By this liturgical action with the chrism, "come and abide" is precisely what the Holy Spirit does for this new member of the Church. "All who have received chrismation," observes contemporary nun Mother Maria Rule, "have had their every opening and member sealed by the gift of the Holy Spirit. We are all therefore Spirit-bearers."[68]

With her damp hair falling over her shoulders and the warmth of oil adorning her softly, Catherine remembers something she learned in one of her catechism classes. What is happening to her, she knows deeply now, is a *symbol*. In fact, the whole sacramental life of the Orthodox Church is symbolic. Catherine discovered, however, that even her understanding of what a symbol is had to be transformed.

Catherine learned in catechism that a symbol—from the Greek word *symbolon*—often means, "a joining of two realities in which neither reality is diminished." A symbol can refer to a sacrament that joins a heavenly reality, such as the grace of the Holy Spirit, with a physical reality, such as the oil of anointing.

In class, Catherine's priest tried to explain that this understanding of the sacraments as symbols flows from a precise understanding of the incarnation of Jesus Christ, who is Divine Nature and human nature in one Person: as He was described in the fifth-century Council of Chalcedon, Christ is "perfect in Godhead and perfect in humanity, truly God and truly human, acknowledged in two Natures *without confusion, without change, without division, without separation*."

One Person, two Natures. From this union flows the very possibility of humanity's union with God. And it places the sacraments of the Church in their proper and wondrous light—by the grace and goodwill of God, spiritual and uncreated and divine realities are joined with material and created and human realities, and these are joined: *without confusion*—each reality remains distinct; *without change*—each reality remains what it is; *without division*—the two realities are truly united; *without separation*—the two realities are truly joined. When Catherine was baptized, the water remained water while mystically joined with the death and resurrection of Christ; when she was chrismated, the oil remained oil while mystically imparting the grace of the Holy Spirit. That chrismation, as Tertullian described it, was a *physical experience*—"the oil runs over the body"—that imparted a *spiritual reality*—"but it profits us spiritually."

And in the Holy Communion that Catherine will soon receive, bread and wine will remain bread and wine while mystically joined with the body and blood of Christ. This and every sacramental joining of spiritual and physical is accomplished by the compassionate descent of the Holy Spirit.

Even as the priest is applying the chrism to Catherine's hands and feet, she recalls that this understanding of symbol had been a revelation to her. She had always assumed that a symbol had only one meaning: a symbol was a *substitute*, something that *stands in* for something else. Symbols created not unity but division; because something is *this*, it therefore is not *that*. Catherine remembered a Greek woman in her new church mentioning that the opposite of *symbolic* is *diabolic*, which means "to divide or fragment or tear apart."

Catherine is holding a candle now, wrapped in lace with a small silver cross affixed to it and prepared lovingly for her by the priest's wife. The flame lightens a faint oil image of a cross on the back of Catherine's hand. Now the hard part begins.

While chrismation is the initial event for Orthodox Christians by which the Holy Spirit will "come and abide in us," becoming a *permanent* home of the Holy Spirit is our calling for life. This is why the prayer to the Holy Spirit, serving as our narrative guide, can be offered every single day. We ask Him to "come and abide in us," filling every breath and guiding every circumstance. As Catherine will learn, the real struggle for salvation begins after the chrism dries.

The priest now offers a prayer that gives Catherine a sense of protection and reassurance for the journey of salvation:

O Thou Who, through holy Baptism, hast given unto Thy servant remission of sins, and hast bestowed upon her a life of regeneration: Do Thou, the same Lord and Master, ever graciously illumine her heart with the light of Thy countenance. Maintain the shield of her faith unassailed by the enemy. Preserve pure and unpolluted the garment of incorruption, wherewith Thou hast endowed her, upholding inviolate in her by Thy grace, the seal of the Spirit, keep her ever a warrior invincible in every attack of those who assail her and us; and make us all victors, even unto the end, through Thy crown incorruptible.

Once the Holy Spirit has come to abide within the newly baptized, the task remains to never drive Him away. Here the struggle of the Christian life begins. Catherine is to "preserve pure and unpolluted the garment of incorruption" she has just received in baptism. This preservation is the profound life of repentance that prepares the soul for eternity with God.

To help her grow in this new life, Catherine will have much support: the sacrament of confession, where she will confess her failings to God in the presence of a spiritual father; a full liturgical life, where she will both receive nourishment and offer intercessions; a rich tradition, from which she may glean the experiences of faithful men and women in ages past; her parish family, with whom she will learn how to love, to serve, to forgive, to persevere; the poor, through whom Christ will pull her out of herself and her selfishness.

Most importantly, Catherine will have the Eucharist: "It helps the initiate after their Initiation," observes the fourteenth-century writer Saint Nicholas Cabasilas, in his classic work *Life in Christ*, "when the ray of light derived from the Sacred Mysteries must be revived after being obscured by the darkness of sin. To revive those who fade away and die because of their sins is the work of the Sacred Table alone."[69] Baptism and chrismation happen once, but our habitual falls into sin and our constant need for transformation render Holy Communion a lifelong necessity. Indeed, there is *always* more of the Holy Spirit to acquire and *always* more of the self to yield.

When an Orthodox Christian reflects back on the day of his chrismation—years later, perhaps—the humble soul will not wonder at how easily he was given the Holy Spirit. Rather, he will wonder at how easily he drove the Holy Spirit away. Sin, however slight, corrupts the "garment of incorruption" and can, to use New Testament language, "quench" (1 Thess. 5:19), "grieve" (Eph. 4:30), "insult" (Heb. 10:20), even "blaspheme" (Matt. 12:31–32) the Holy Spirit. While chrismation is our first full indwelling of the Holy Spirit, repentance is the struggle to overcome the sin with which the Holy Spirit cannot abide.

This calls to mind *Adam's Lament*, a chapter from a book on Catherine's reading list. Written by Saint Silouan of Mount Athos, *Adam's Lament* is a poetic reflection on what the biblical Adam experienced when he sinned against God and was expelled from Paradise. Saint Silouan gives to Adam a voice of the most profound pain; a voice of anguish because he lost so completely what he had once enjoyed so fully—communion with God. Adam lost Paradise, but it is not Paradise for which he yearns—the greenery, the richness of Eden, the lush life of the Garden. Instead, the perfection of Paradise is worse than pollution when compared with the communion with God in the Holy Spirit that he used to enjoy—*that* is why he sorrows.

Adam, father of all mankind, in paradise knew the sweetness of the love of God; and so when, for his sin, he was driven forth from the Garden of Eden, and was widowed of the love of God, he suffered grievously and lamented with a mighty moan. And the whole desert rang with his lamentation. His soul was racked as he thought: "I have grieved my beloved Lord." He sorrowed less after paradise and the beauty thereof—he sorrowed that he was bereft of the love of God, which insatiably, at every instant, draws the soul to Him.

In the same way, the soul which has known God through the Holy Spirit but has afterwards lost grace, experiences the torment that Adam suffered. There is an aching and a deep regret in the soul that has grieved the beloved Lord.

Adam pined on earth, and wept bitterly, and the earth was not pleasing to him. He was heartsick for God, and this was his cry:

"My soul wearies for the Lord, and I seek Him in tears. How should I not seek Him? When I was with Him my soul was glad and at rest, and the enemy could not come nigh me. But now the spirit of evil has gained power over me, harassing and oppressing my soul . . ."

The soul of Adam fell sick when he was exiled from paradise, and many were the tears he shed in his distress. Likewise, every soul that has known the Lord yearns for Him, and cries.

The Holy Spirit is love and sweetness for the soul, mind, and body. And those who have come to know God by the Holy Spirit stretch upward day and night, insatiable, to the living God, for the love of God is exceedingly sweet. But when the soul loses grace, her tears flow as she seeks the Holy Spirit anew.

O Adam we are thy children! Tell us in our tribulation how we may inherit paradise!

Why cry out to me, my children? The Lord loveth you and hath given you commandments. Be faithful to them, love one another, and ye shall find rest in God. Let not an hour pass without repenting of your sins, that ye may be ready to meet the Lord.[70]

In line after line of *Adam's Lament*, we hear the frantic voice of one who had enjoyed communion with God in the Holy Spirit only to lose that communion after having grieved the Holy Spirit. And the feeling from such loss is of a much different magnitude than the feeling from losing a toy or a gift or a job, or even a loved one. "The soul that has lost grace," Saint Silouan writes, "yearns after the Lord, and weeps as Adam wept when he was driven from paradise. And no one can afford her consolation, save God. Adam wept great tears and they ran down in torrents, wetting his countenance, his bosom and the earth beneath his feet; and he fetched deep, powerful sighs like the bellows of a blacksmith. 'Lord, Lord,' he lamented, 'take me into paradise again.' "[71]

The call to the Holy Spirit to "come and abide" is both an event and a process: He comes and abides in the sacramental life of the Church, but the Christian also lives in a state of perpetual yearning to be "taken into paradise again," a yearning lived out in quiet, patient, daily repentance. Such a soul is never truly satisfied but always desires deeper and deeper communion with the divine.

Such deepening communion leaves increasingly little room for the sinful self and its appetites. The story is told of a man who relocated to a new area. While driving in his car one day, he set his radio on "scan." He wanted to get a sense of what the area had to offer. The radio stations were each given about ten seconds before the radio would move on to the next available station. He paused on one station that kept referring to itself as "free radio" and aired brief interviews with people on the street, asking them what "freedom" meant to them. Responses included: "freedom means nobody telling me what to do"; "freedom means doing what I want, when I want, however I want"; "freedom means me calling the shots"; and, as one woman said, "freedom means always being happy."

The interviewer apparently did not ask Mother Gavrilia about freedom. If he had, this saintly nun, who died in 1992 and whose life is recorded in *The Ascetic of Love*, would have offered a decidedly different perspective. "True freedom," Mother Gavrilia used to say, "is freedom from yourself."[72]

The saints talk often about the soul and its desire to take flight. They say that we are made by a God who placed deep within us a kind of sacred restlessness; we are designed to be unsettled *until* we settle in Him, on His word, in His ways. "Come and abide in us" is the constant, natural cry of the soul. "You, O Lord, have created us for Yourself," wrote Saint Augustine, "and we are not at rest until we rest in You."[73]

But while the soul naturally yearns for its Maker; the flesh does not. The flesh is not evil but does exert a kind of downward pressure on the soul, keeping it bound to the pleasures of this world. The soul desires flight toward heaven, but the fallen nature is the hand that grips us around the ankles, keeping us down and distracted. The soul wants God, but the flesh settles for pride; the soul wants God, but the flesh settles for lust; the soul wants God, but the flesh settles for gluttony or anger or jealousy or sloth. Too often we feel it is not the soul that defines us but the flesh. We become identified by our sins. *That* is what Mother Gavrilia had in mind when she said, "True freedom is freedom from yourself." The freedom for which we yearn is the freedom to escape the hand of our sins that grips the soul and keeps it down; it is the freedom to be who God made us to be.

Catherine's baptism and chrismation proclaims to Catherine and all those present that her new life—from the Father, through the Son, in the Holy Spirit, of the Church—must always revolve around the central mystery of what has just happened. Her fallen nature must always be put to death, her new nature always rising. And she must daily join her voice to the choir that, through the ages, calls upon the Holy Spirit to "come and abide in us."

8
Cleanse Us from Every Impurity, and Save our Souls

O heavenly King, the Comforter, the Spirit of truth, Who art everywhere present and fillest all things; Treasury of good things and Giver of life; come and abide in us, and cleanse us from every impurity, and save our souls, O Gracious Lord.

•

*T*he Holy Spirit cleanses, renews, transforms. He dwells within the human being, and we become something that we could never become without Him: pure.

In many steel mills can be found a large bucket called a *crucible*, capable of holding hundreds of gallons of whatever is poured into it. Much of what a steel mill pulls from the earth is dumped into a crucible and placed over a fire. The fire heats the crucible until the contents are boiling, causing impurities to rise to the top. The steelworkers cool the fire down and skim the impurities off the top of what's inside the crucible. Then the crucible is again heated, more impurities rise, and the surface is again skimmed. This process is repeated until all that remains in the crucible is *pure* steel.

Spiritual life is like that. Every person is a crucible, and during times of struggle or testing—when the fire comes—the impurities within us rise to the surface of awareness. When things don't go our way, maybe we grow angry; when offended, maybe resentful; when hurt, bitter. Conflict exposes the content of the heart.

"Do not fear the conflict," wrote the great bishop Saint John Chrysostom, "do not flee it. Where there is no struggle, there is no virtue; where faith and love are not tempted, it is not possible to be sure whether they are really present. They are proved and revealed in adversity."[74] A life without struggle might be comfortable for the flesh, but it is caustic to the soul. The impurities remain within, undetected because no conflict has brought them to the surface. We're dying inside and don't even know it.

This rising of impurities is one reason why the Christian monastic tradition in particular lays great emphasis on not leaving a place or life situation easily. One fourth-century Desert Mother, Saint Syncletica, offered this image: "If you find yourself in a monastic community, do not pick up and go to another place, for that will harm you a great deal. Just as the bird who abandons the eggs on which she was sitting prevents them from hatching, so the monk or nun grows cold in their faith and dies, when they flit from one place to another."

Monk or nun, but also parishioner or husband or employee or team member or friend. The shine of a new situation or a new setting or new people is one of the joys of life, but it usually wears off with time; and that's when the real soul work begins. Egos bump egos, the habits of one collide with the habits of another, or life simply gets grim with anything from car trouble to a cancer scare, and the flames under the crucible of each heart are kindled. To leave a situation or a place or a person when the temperature gets uncomfortable might mean abandoning whatever good was growing there—those "eggs" that may be on the verge of hatching, to use Saint Syncletica's image. Certainly, however, there are times when conflict becomes unbearable and staying put would do more harm than moving on.

When conflict with other persons brings our impurities to the surface, those persons become—if we have the courage to see them in this way—angels of healing. They bring to our awareness the internal toxins keeping us from becoming saints. We see these persons critically if we believe they're the real problem, but we may see them appreciatively if we believe they're revealing the real problem within ourselves. This deep interior cleansing, often at the hands of the most irritating people, is the work of the Holy Spirit.

Happily, there are times when the conflicts of life reveal pure elements rising from within us to the surface of our conscious thoughts and behaviors—patience or love or humility or contentment—and this is evidence that the Holy Spirit has been at work in us. We then take special solace in the possibility that we can be peacemakers. Other times, however, we discover impurities—irritability or anger or pride or lust for power—and this is evidence that the Holy Spirit has yet to fully, as the prayer to Him says, "cleanse us from every impurity, and save our souls."

Pure or impure, the contents of the crucible of the heart are revealed in times of conflict. And if the prophet Jeremiah is correct—that "the heart is deceitful above all things, and desperately wicked" (Jer. 17:9 NKJV)—what usually comes to surface during conflict are qualities unworthy of a child of God. The rising to awareness, then, is a *gift*. The longer we are not aware of the impurities within us—the ones that simmer beneath the surface of consciousness—the greater chance they have of damaging lives. We beg the Holy Spirit to "cleanse us from every impurity" because such cleansing is an act of mercy not only on ourselves but also upon all those with whom we come into contact. For a deeper appreciation for how the content of one heart affects the condition of another, let's move from the steel mill to the shipyard.

Until the 1950s, there lived on the western Pacific island of Guam many native species of birds—birds of all sizes and colors, all unique to Guam. Just a few decades later, however, many of those species were extinct. Their extinction was not due to some bird virus or plague. Instead, as culture on Guam developed, trading ships began making the island a regular stop on their routes to drop off and pick up various goods. Some of those ships came from places like Australia and Papua New Guinea and were loaded with cargo that attracted a particular kind of snake from those lands—the brown tree snake.

Deep in the hulls of the ships, below the waterline and lurking among the dark spaces, these brown tree snakes lived comfortably. When the trading ships docked at the new ports in Guam, over time, the brown tree snakes found their way onto land. And what they found there was, for a snake, paradise: an unlimited supply of bird eggs and no natural predators. As a result, this hidden, invasive animal spread everywhere and permanently damaged not just the bird population of Guam but its ecology, its commerce, even its human health. Above the waterline, the ships were beautiful, like floating signs of progress and prosperity; below the waterline, however, they carried something destructive that no one could see but was really there, and its devastation spread far beyond its secret habitat.

"For nothing is secret that will not be revealed," Jesus said, "nor anything hidden that will not be known and come to light" (Luke 8:17). Every human being is a ship at sea. We carry lots of things that make up our *conscious* selves: habits, memories, preferences, ways of thinking and feeling and living and relating to other people. These are the individual qualities that we are aware of; this is our life above the waterline.

But this is not all there is to us. We also carry lots of cargo beneath the waterline—those things that make up our deep, inner selves: an emotional past, psychological habits, old tapes that play in our subconscious; and all of this is every bit a part of us as are our conscious selves. These subconscious elements can be like snakes on a ship—something destructive that no one can see but is really there, and their devastation can spread far beyond their secret habitat.

What happens, then, when we enter into a relationship with another person? When in relationship—husband and wife, parent and child, siblings or coworkers or teammates or friends or acquaintances or even strangers in a brief encounter—we are naturally preoccupied with what lies above the waterline. This is all the stuff that passes on the surface—conversations, ideas, hobbies, ways of communicating, ways of relating, shared joys and shared sorrows.

But that is not all that leaves the ship of the self. Here we reach the "deceitful heart" of which the prophet Jeremiah wrote. Beneath the waterline lie deep broken places that we don't think are there but that come out of us anyway: fears, old habits, buried resentments, wounds that never healed and sins that were never cleansed. These are very real, and they pass from us to those with whom we come into contact. Every relationship is the merging of two pasts, like two diaries coming together. Eventually we are going to feel every entry.

There is a deep and ancient Christian explanation for why we hurt those we love and are hurt by those who love us: everyone of us is a *psychopath*. We do not mean this in some clinical or criminal sense. Instead, we mean precisely what the word itself means: the word *psychopath* comes from two Greek and biblical words—*psyche*, which means "soul," and *pathos* which means "suffering." A "psychopath," then, is a "suffering soul," and every soul suffers in some way.

The soul suffers from sin, from neglect, from indifference. These work their way through the body, like poison through soil, to infect the deep self and cause deep inner suffering. But this suffering does not stay there. Because the human being is an organic whole—mind, body, and soul in unity—whatever lies below the waterline works its way out beyond its ship and onto the island of another person. We *want* to be good to each other; we *try* to be good to each other; and so much that passes from one person to another *is* good and true and beautiful.

But it is a spiritual principle that every snake not purged from the ship finds its way out: words we wish we could take back; deeds we wish we had left undone; patterns of communication that don't nurture but damage unity; personal sins that are not so personal after all. Our interior condition effects others, and this is one reason why we may continually beg the Holy Spirit to "cleanse us from every impurity."

This awareness of how our inner condition affects others is also why the Orthodox Church places such emphasis on ascetic striving and personal repentance. Christian repentance is not simply a turning away from evil but also a tightening embrace of good, and it invites the grace of God below the waterline. This is why true repentance changes more than just external behavior; it changes the deep self—the inner person from whom all behaviors flow.

The saints tell us that this internal cleansing is the greatest gift we can give to another person. Elder Paisios of Mount Athos, in his book *With Pain and Love for Contemporary Man*, writes this:

Spiritual work on ourselves is actually a silent work on our fellow human beings. . . . Whatever work we do on our spiritual life should not be considered a waste of time. We may need to work for a short while or for a long time, even for a lifetime, but the important thing is to work, because this mystical labor will preach the word of God mystically into the souls of people. It liberates them from the tyranny of the passions and, in so doing, brings them closer to God where they find salvation.[75]

Conflict will come, and with it comes a growing awareness of the world within us. Every human being is a ship that sails toward others, and a clean vessel—both above and below the waterline—is the great gift we can bring. Repentance is the highest act of love.

The sacrament of repentance is another name for the sacrament of confession—that *sacred space* where Orthodox Christians beg God to unload all the toxic cargo we've been carrying. Archaeological digs of Christian catacombs have uncovered mosaics with images of the bodies of Christians at worship—standing upright with outstretched arms. This too is the perpetual posture of the soul as it calls daily on the Holy Spirit to "cleanse us from every impurity." And this yearning gives rise to regular visits to the "sacred space" of confession, where a "broken and a contrite heart" (Ps. 51:17 NKJV) lays itself bare before God in the presence of a priest who can encourage, shepherd, and pronounce God's forgiveness to the penitent in a tangible way. In this way, confession is more about God's love than it is about our sins.

Confession restores communion. There is no communion with God without asking for His forgiveness for all we have done, and do, to sever that communion. And because the confessions of sin in Holy Scripture occur in the presence of another person, an angel, the incarnate Lord, or the congregation of Israel, the relational component of confession is horizontal as well as vertical. That accountability helps toward making sure our contrition shows up in our behavior; saying "I'm sorry" means little if I'm not dealing with what I say I'm sorry for. This may be why repentance may be a better name for the sacrament: repentance means, "to turn the whole of a person—thought, word, deed—around."

In its fullest meaning, repentance is more than the spring cleaning of the soul. The prayer to the Holy Spirit calls upon Him to "cleanse us from every impurity, *and* save our souls." We have touched on the cleansing of impurities, but what might the prayer mean when it refers to the salvation of souls? Here we discover that the goal of Christian life is much more than becoming a crucible cleansed of its waste or a ship purged of its snakes.

Salvation involves what a person is being saved *to* as much as it involves what a person is being saved *from*. Some people might think of salvation as what happens "by the skin of your teeth." That is to say, a person is saved from shipwrecks and car crashes, from dangerous situations and near misses. The very question, "What must I do to be saved?" implies this idea of *escape*, as in, "What must I do to escape hell, condemnation, eternal suffering, endless misery?" Hiding in this approach may be a more subtle question, "What is the least I must do to be saved?" This is an attitude of *minimalism*.

While escape from punishment may be part of salvation as described in Holy Scripture, it is nowhere near the whole. Consider, for example, the Sermon on the Mount. Nowhere in this glorious instruction did Christ say *be saved*. Instead, the culmination of His sermon is *be perfect*. "You shall be perfect, just as your Father in heaven is perfect" (Matt. 5:48).

The "salvation of our souls" as found in the prayer to the Holy Spirit, then, is a much more exalted, more glorious, even more rigorous process than the mere escape from condemnation. Instead, we may understand salvation as *perfection in God*.

To be cleansed of every impurity and to be saved in soul, as the prayer states, means not only that we stop doing sinful things but also that we actually become holy; not only that we stop falling into old habits but also that we actually become new creations; not only that we not judge but also that we actually become mercy; not only not condemn but also become love; not only not complain but also become joy; not only that we change on the level of *behavior*—refraining from displeasing God—but also that we change on the level of *desire*—wanting to please God.

The Orthodox view of salvation is more than merely getting by, more than merely doing enough. Instead, salvation is a positive and never-ending process of personal transfiguration in God, a process impossible without the indwelling of the Holy Spirit of God. For the Orthodox Christian—whether born into the faith as a child or drawn to the faith as an adult—that indwelling of the Holy Spirit for the "salvation of souls" will unfold with frequent participation not only in the sacrament of confession but also in the most exalted sacrament of Holy Communion.

In the consecrated bread and wine of Holy Communion, the very life of Christ becomes our very life. We recall that just as the greenery of Pentecost eventually browns, biological life eventually dies. The seed of eternal life sown within us by personal faith and Church baptism must be watered by a lifestyle worthy of such eternity—the baptized must also become the obedient, the faithful, the martyr; and this is our *imitation* of Christ. The new life begun in baptism, so easily wilted through neglect, will also continue to grow through faithful, careful, thoughtful reception of Holy Communion, and this is our *participation* in Christ.

As the priest prepares the chalice of Holy Communion, he pours hot water into the wine, saying, "the warmth of faith, full of the Holy Spirit." This warmth will reach the recipient on a visceral level as Holy Communion stirs with the temperature of life. Because the warmth brings the energy of fire, "it signifies the Holy Spirit," observed Saint Nicholas Cabasilas, "Who came down upon the Apostles in the form of fire."[76]

In Holy Communion, the Holy Spirit—who descended to transform the Apostles into vessels of the Church; the water of baptism into a vessel of life-giving death; the oil of chrismation into a vessel of divine grace; the sacred space of confession into a vessel for the cleansing from sin; and, indeed, who descends to transform the physical universe itself into a vessel of spiritual realities—descends to transform bread and wine into the body and blood of Christ, who is "the way, the truth, and the life" and without whom no one comes to the Father (John 14:6). Then, from cup to communicant, transformation occurs in the greatest physical universe of all—the human being.

How does the salvation imparted in Holy Communion actually adorn a person? The prayers that an Orthodox Christian offers around his participation in the sacrament—often called *pre-Communion* and *post-Communion* prayers—provide a glimpse into how the Holy Spirit comes to "save our souls" in this mystical supper. The list reads like a rhapsody.

For those who worthily receive, the *Holy Mysteries* provide communion of the Holy Spirit; provision for the journey of eternal life; an acceptable answer at the dread judgment seat of Christ; sanctification; enlightenment and strengthening of soul and body; relief from the burden of many transgressions; protection against every action of the devil; repulsion and victory over wicked and evil habits; mortification of passions;

accomplishment of Christ's commandments; increase of divine grace; inheritance of Christ's kingdom; sanctity for soul and body, mind and heart, muscles and bones; a place at Christ's right hand with the saved; purification and healing; a promise of the life and Kingdom to come; a defense and a help and a repulsion of every attacker; the removal of many transgressions; enlightenment and healing; repulsion of every tempting thought and action of the devil; boldness and love for Christ; correction and grounding of life; increase of virtue and perfection; fulfillment of Christ's commandments; enlivening and deifying of all who partake with a pure heart; enlightenment and salvation of the world; full participation in Christ's Divinity; the Lover of humankind living within; enlightenment of darkened reasoning; uniting with the ranks of the friends of Christ; perfect removal and destruction of evil thoughts, reasonings, intentions, and fantasies; enlightening of spiritual senses; burning up of spiritual faults; healing of soul and body; repelling of every adversary; illumining of the eyes of the heart; peace of one's spiritual powers; a faith unashamed; a genuine love; fulfilling of wisdom; receiving of divine grace; illumination of one's five senses; joy, health, and gladness.

All of this is but a fraction of the fullness of divine life imparted in the whole sacramental experience of the Church—a fullness that can never be described, explained, or exhausted. Such fullness ultimately speaks to the astonishing condescension of the Holy Trinity—"the grace of the Lord Jesus Christ, and the love of God, and the communion of the Holy Spirit" (2 Cor. 13:14). Rising to meet this condescension is the singular pursuit of the *crucible* desiring to be pure and the *ship* yearning to be cleansed.

9
O Gracious Lord

O heavenly King, the Comforter, the Spirit of truth, Who art
everywhere present and fillest all things; Treasury of good
things and Giver of life; come and abide in us, and cleanse
us from every impurity, and save our souls, O Gracious Lord.

•

RACE. HOW CAN IT BE both a simple prayer
before meals and the uncreated energy of
almighty God? And how can crude finite
creatures begin to comprehend this, His most
incomprehensible trait? He is so wholly *other*, so clear of every
conceivable concept or analogy, so beyond earth's every form and
void. And yet, grace descends. Grace descends upon the child at
breakfast and the theologian in thought, upon both the inhabited
and the uninhabited world. God is the "Good One," as a better
translation of "Gracious Lord" calls Him, who sends the grace of
Himself and comes to bear on everything that has being, on what
Shakespeare's Hamlet called "this quintessence of dust."[77]

Those of us who cannot approach an understanding of grace
can at least gain an appreciation for it, not through constructing
a theory but through considering a person—a woman, described
by an ancient hymn as "full of grace":

Rejoice, O Virgin, Theotokos, Mary, full of grace, the Lord is with thee; blessed art thou among women, and blessed is the fruit of thy womb, for thou hast born the Savior of our souls.

This hymn is based on the Archangel Gabriel's announcement to Mary, recorded in the first chapter of Saint Luke's Gospel, that she was no ordinary woman and this was no ordinary grace:

Mary . . . you have found favor with God. And behold, you will conceive in your womb and bring forth a Son, and shall call His name JESUS. He will be great, and will be called the Son of the Highest; and the Lord God will give Him the throne of His father David. And He will reign over the house of Jacob forever, and of His kingdom there will be no end. . . .

. . . The Holy Spirit will come upon you, and the power of the Highest will overshadow you; therefore, also, that Holy One who is to be born will be called the Son of God. (Luke 1:30–33, 35)

So exalted is the example of Mary that Orthodox Christians prefer to let the Holy Spirit do the talking. As we sing most Sunday mornings in the service of Matins, "I shall open my mouth and it will be filled with the Spirit, and I shall speak forth to the Queen and Mother."[78]

The mystery of this pure Jewish maiden "full of grace" can be found among the deeper richness of the Bible—the "treasure hidden in a field" of Holy Scripture (Matt. 13:44). And what emerges from the rich biblical portrait of Mary are clues about the grace and goodness of the Holy Spirit and counsel for all who yearn to acquire His grace and goodness for themselves.

First, a few brushstrokes from the biblical portrait of she who is full of grace: among other places, *types* or *prefigurings* of Mary may be found in Genesis 28, as the angelic ladder that Jacob beholds bridging heaven and earth—a type of her who becomes the bridge where the heavenly God comes to dwell on earth; in Exodus 16, as the golden dish of Moses that holds the precious manna—a type of her who holds Him within whom is the Bread of Life; in Numbers 17, as the staff of Aaron that blossoms forth a bud that has no seed—a type of her who blossomed forth the God-Man without seed; in Psalm 45, as the "queen arrayed in a robe of gold"—a type of her who clothed herself in the golden robe of humility and became the physical "palace" for the "King"; and in Ezekiel 44, as the gate through which the King passed, the gate then closed off to every other man—a type of the ever-virginity of her who became the Gate through which God passed into our world, the gate then closed off forever. The fragrance of Mary, as does the aroma of the Holy Trinity, rises from the early pages of sacred Scripture.

To those who yearn to be filled with the grace of the Holy Spirit, the "gracious Lord," it is significant that all of these Old Testament references prefigure Mary as an *empty vessel*—as a ladder awaiting crossing; a dish awaiting manna; a staff awaiting blossoming; a Queen awaiting her King; a gate awaiting one single and exceptional passing. When the archangel Gabriel encountered Mary, he found a vessel thoroughly emptied of anything unworthy of the Holy Spirit, who would soon overshadow her. Mary reveals that any who strive for grace must be emptied of all defilements that leave less, if any, room for grace.

Grace for the Orthodox is not some pleasant vibration from above but the very real presence of the Holy Spirit. As the power and activity of God in creation, grace is not something He creates but something He *is*. The Good One pours His grace into us, so that He shares not only what He has, but what He is: "All that I have is yours," said the father to the prodigal son; "All that I Am is yours," says God to His children. His grace indwells the empty vessel and pours forth in word, deed, thought, and appearance. These vessels—full, paradoxically, as long as they remain empty—become lights to the world and cities set on a hill, which cannot be hid (Matt. 5:14).

"To possess grace," wrote Saint Silouan of Mount Athos, who continues this theme of becoming a worthy receptacle, "one must be temperate in all things—in his gestures, in speech, in what he lets his eyes look upon, in his thoughts, in the food he eats. And every form of temperance is furthered by meditation in the word of God." By "temperance," Saint Silouan means "moderation" or "self-restraint." He means "empty."

Notice the saint's practical counsel. To possess grace, we begin by emptying ourselves of gestures that are unseemly or inappropriate; of speech that is idle or ugly or unnecessary; of images that inflame passions; of thoughts that clog or prevent prayer; and as for food, "we must train ourselves to eat as little as possible, yet within reason, as our work permits. After meals," the saint continues, "we should feel like praying—that is the measure of moderation."[79]

This emptying of all that may repel the Holy Spirit helps each of us become the "clean vessel" for use by the Lord of which the prophet Isaiah spoke (Isa. 66:20 NKJV), and begins the process of our beautification. Grace is beautiful, and the more grace we acquire the more beautiful we become. In another beloved hymn about Mary, the archangel Gabriel stands astonished by her equal measure of grace and beauty:

Awed by the beauty of thy virginity, and the exceeding radiance of thy purity, Gabriel stood amazed and cried to thee, O Mother of God: "What praise may I offer thee that is worthy of thy beauty? By what name shall I call thee? I am lost and bewildered. But I shall greet thee as I was commanded: 'Rejoice, thou who art full of grace.' "[80]

Modern ideas about beauty and virginity depend on narrow, trendy definitions: beauty is defined by appearance and shape; virginity by deprivation and lack. Beauty is understood as what the body has; virginity as what the body has not. But these modern ideas fall far short of the rich wholeness of the beauty and virginity rooted in the indwelling grace of the Holy Spirit. If Gabriel was "awed by the beauty" of Mary's virginity, it may have been because of the radiance released from her total and expansive union with God, a pure union uncompromised by any lesser union with another human being. This radiance is only possible for a vessel emptied of all other lights of love and fires of passion.

Single or married, rich or poor, old or young, fettered with responsibilities or free from cares—the grace of the Holy Spirit beautifies all empty vessels in ways unique to each. Saint Silouan noticed that the inner mystery of grace is observable in outward changes:

I once knew a boy who looked like an angel. He was submissive and gentle. His little face was pink and white; his clear blue eyes shone kind and tranquil. But when he grew up he began to lead a bad life, and lost the grace of God; and so by the time he reached the age of thirty, he looked a mixture of man and devil, wild beast and cut-throat, and the whole appearance of him was ruthless and dreadful.

I knew a girl, too, who was very beautiful—her face was so radiant and lovely that many were envious of her beauty. But through sin she lost grace, and then it was painful to look at her.

But I have also seen the reverse. I have seen men arrive in the Monastery with faces disfigured by sin and passion, but with repentance and a devout life they changed and became good to look upon.

Another time the Lord let me see a priest, as he stood hearing confessions, in the image of Christ. Though his hair was white with age, his face looked young and beautiful like the face of a boy, so inexpressibly radiant was he.

Thus sin disfigures a man while grace beautifies him.[81]

Such beautification cannot be forced or coerced, nor is it a feeling of goodwill that we churn out or an affect that we take on. The Russian term for grace—*blagodat*—is a combination of words meaning "goodness" and "given." Grace is an indwelling gift from the Good One, for "every good gift and every perfect gift is from above, and comes down from the Father of lights" (Jas. 1:17).

This gift of grace, as it did most supremely for Mary, carries the worthy to their own unfathomable heights. Here the Holy Spirit in Orthodox tradition begins to emerge in His full glory: the grace of the Holy Spirit does not return humanity to the Eden from where we were exiled but leads us to somewhere incomparably higher.

The saving work of Christ has reconciled a fallen world with the Father, and Eden has been opened for all. Now, however, humanity can do more than walk with God in the garden. In the Holy Spirit, all empty vessels are led toward a state more glorious than that communion with God enjoyed by Adam and Eve.

In Eden, we dwelled with Him who is eternal, immortal, everlasting; but in the Holy Spirit, we *become* eternal, immortal, everlasting. Remaining created, we transcend the created. We slip the bonds of mortality, with its manifold limitations, and dwell—*now*—in a state where prayer is life and the miraculous is normal. For the saintly few, this blessed state is their present reality. For most of us, however, such blessedness is the pursuit of a lifetime, the patient and prolonged walk through the "narrow gate" (Matt. 7:13).

"The Holy Spirit heals us from the consequences of the fall, regenerates us and hallows us," wrote Father Sophrony Sakharov, a spiritual son of Saint Silouan. "But all this He accomplishes in an invisible manner, like some marvelous diffident Friend Who does not want to burden us with gratitude to Him. The great blessedness of knowing Him comes gradually."[82]

Gradually, the Holy Spirit leads the truly willing—and, therefore, regrettably rare—soul through the struggle of purification, the sweetness of illumination, and the grace of perfection, until all that remains is union with God—the highest, most exalted, yet most natural state for which the human being was created. This is the life for which we were made; this is the life of the saints.

The eyes of humanity have not seen, nor have our ears heard, nor has it even entered into our hearts the things God has prepared for those who love Him. Yet, in the astonishing condescension of God, the Holy Spirit reveals them all (1 Cor. 2:9–11). When the grace of the Good One descends, sorrows are quieted and minds are cleared, light dispels darkness and the faculties of humanity are rightly ordered.

When grace descends, the world is granted a glimpse of what is possible with God:

Abba Lot went to see Abba Joseph and said to him, "Abba, as far as I can, I say my little office, I fast a little, I pray and meditate, I live in peace, and as far as I can, I purify my thoughts. What else can I do?" Then the old man stood up and stretched his hands toward heaven. His fingers became like ten lamps of fire and he said to him, "If you will, you can become all flame."[83]

Notes

PREFACE

1 St. Symeon the New Theologian, *Hymns of Divine Love*, trans. George A. Maloney (Denville, NJ: Dimension, 1976), 9.

INTRODUCTION

2 St. Nikolai Velimirovich, *Homilies* (Birmingham, UK: Lazarica Press, 1996), 1:306.

3 St. Gregory of Nyssa, *The Life of Moses* (San Francisco: HarperSan-Francisco, 2006), xx. [AQ: Please provide page number.]

4 Vespers of Pentecost.

5 A better translation of "Gracious Lord" is "Good One." Compare Matthew 7:11 with Luke 11:13, and notice the connection between the "good things" God gives to His children and the "Holy Spirit" who is the one given.

6 St. Isaac of Syria *Treatises* xx. [AQ: Please provide chapter and/or paragraph numbers.]

CHAPTER 1

7 An example of this is the prophet David's joyful song after emerging victorious from battles with Saul and the Philistines, as recorded in 2 Samuel 22:1–23:7.

8 St. Basil the Great, *On the Holy Spirit*, trans. David Anderson (Crestwood, NY: St. Vladimir's Seminary Press, 1980), 16.

9 Ibid., 28.

10 Ibid., 73.

11 Ibid., 85.

12 Ibid., 87.

13 From the Anaphora of the Divine Liturgy of St. Basil.

14 St. Basil the Great *Epistle* 214.4.

15 St. Symeon the New Theologian, *Hymns of Divine Love*, trans. George A. Maloney (Denville, NJ: Dimension, 1976), 39.

16 Exaposteilarion of Matins of Pentecost.

17 Praises of Matins of Pentecost.

18 St. Gregory of Nyssa, in his essay *On Not Three Gods*, provides this classic expression of the how the Holy Trinity relates to the world.

19 St. Gregory of Sinai *Texts on Commandments and Dogmas* 30.

20 St. Gregory of Nyssa *Letter* 38.

21 St. Basil, *On the Holy Spirit*, 28.

22 St. Gregory the Theologian, *On God and Christ*, trans. Frederick Williams and Lionel Wickham (Crestwood, NY: St. Vladimir's Seminary Press, 2002), 137.

23 Vespers of Pentecost.

CHAPTER 2

24 Dionysios Farasiotis, *The Gurus, the Young Man, and Elder Paisios*, ed. Philip Navarro (Platina, CA: St. Herman Press, 2008), 117–19.

25 St. Theophylact of Bulgaria, *The Explanation of the Holy Gospel According to John* (House Springs, MO: Chrysostom Press, 2007), 230–31.

26 St. Gregory Palamas, *The Saving Work of Christ: Sermons by Saint Gregory Palamas*, ed. Christopher Veniamin (Waymart, PA: Mount Thabor Publishing, 2008), 131.

27 St. Macarius the Great *Spiritual Homilies* 17. Emphasis added.

28 St. John of Kronstadt, *My Life in Christ* ([Place]: [Publisher], [date]) xx. [AQ: Please provide publication info and page number.]

29 Divine Liturgy of St. John Chrysostom. Emphasis added.

30 Elder Paisios of the Holy Mountain, *With Pain and Love for Contemporary Man* (Thessaloniki, Greece: Holy Monastery "Evangelist John the Theologian," 2007), 167–68.

CHAPTER 3

31 Sister Magdalen, *Conversations with Children* (Essex, UK: Patriarchal Stavropegic Monastery of St. John the Baptist, 2004), 196–97.

32 Archimandrite Sophrony Sakharov, *We Shall See Him As He Is* (Essex, UK: Patriarchal Stavropegic Monastery of St. John the Baptist, 2004), 193.

33 Sister Magdalen, *Conversations with Children*, 28.

34 St. Gregory the Theologian *On Theophany, or the Nativity of Christ*, Oration 38.

35 St. Macarius the Great *On God and the Human Soul*, Homily 49.

36 Elisabeth Behr-Sigel, *The Place of the Heart: An Introduction to Orthodox Spirituality* (Torrance, CA: Oakwood Publications, 1992), 1.

37 Archimandrite Sophrony Sakharov, *Saint Silouan the Athonite* (Essex, UK: Patriarchal Stavropegic Monastery of St. John the Baptist, 1991), 388.

38 Jaroslav Pelikan, *Credo* (New Haven, CT: Yale University Press, 2003), 7–34.

39 Sister Magdalen, *Conversations with Children*, 143–44.

CHAPTER 4

40 St. John Chrysostom *On the Incomprehensible Nature of God* 1.19.

41 Evagrius of Pontus, as quoted in Timothy Ware, *The Orthodox Way* (Crestwood, NY: St. Vladimir's Seminary Press, 2003), 11.

42 Anaphora of the Divine Liturgy of St. John Chrysostom.

43 Philip Sherrard, *Christianity: Lineaments of a Sacred Tradition* (Brookline, MA: Holy Cross Orthodox Press, 1998), 239.

44 Vladimir Lossky, *The Mystical Theology of the Eastern Church* (Crestwood, NY: St. Vladimir's Seminary Press, 1976), 69, 70.

45 St. Maximos the Confessor, "First Century on Theology," 50, *The Philokalia*, Volume 2, translated by G. E. H. Palmer, Kallistos Ware and Philip Sherrard, (London, Faber and Faber, 1981), 124.

46 Olivier Clément, *Three Prayers*, trans. Michael Breck (Crestwood, NY: St. Vladimir's Seminary Press, 2000), 50–52.

47 Brenda Meehan, *Holy Women of Russia: The Lives of Five Orthodox Women Offer Spiritual Guidance for Today* (San Francisco: HarperSanFrancisco, 1993), 41.

48 St. John of Kronstadt, *My Life in Christ*, (Jordanville, NY: Holy Trinity Monastery, 1994), 515-16.

49 St. Gregory Palamas, *The Saving Work of Christ: Sermons by Saint Gregory Palamas*, ed. Christopher Veniamin (Waymart, PA: Mount Thabor Publishing, 2008), 134–35.

50 Owen Chadwick, editor, *Western Asceticism*, (Louisville, KY: Westminster John Knox Press, 1958), 188.

51 In Acts 17:8, the apostle Paul is probably quoting the pagan Greek poets Epimenides and Aerates.

52 St. Seraphim of Sarov, ["St. Seraphim of Sarov's Conversation with Nicholas Motovilov"], in *Little Russian Philokaoia*, Vol. 1, Saint Seraphim of Sarov, (Platina, CA: St. Herman of Alaska Brotherhood, 2008), 92.

53 Dionysius Farasiotis, *The Gurus, the Young Man, and Elder Paisios*, ed. Philip Navarro (Platina, CA: St. Herman Press), 292.

CHAPTER 5

54   First Antiphon, Tone 7, Matins.

55   Archimandrite Lazarus Moore, *St. Seraphim of Sarov, A Spiritual Biography*, (Blanco, TX: New Sarov Press, 1994) 126.

56   St. Gregory Palamas, *The Homilies*, ed. and trans. Christopher Veniamin (Waymart, PA: Mount Thabor Publishing, 2009), 194.

57   As recorded in Valentine Zander, *St. Seraphim of Sarov* (Crestwood, NY: St. Vladimir's Seminary Press, 1975), 84–94.

CHAPTER 6

58   St. Gregory of Nyssa *On Virginity* 14.1.

59   St. Cyril of Alexandria *Commentary on the Epistle to the Romans*. [AQ: Please add chapter and/or paragraph number.]

60   St. Cyril of Jerusalem, *Lectures on the Christian Sacraments* (Crestwood, NY: St. Vladimir's Seminary Press, 1977), 61.

61   Timothy Ware, *The Orthodox Church* (London: Penguin, 1963), 274.

62   St. Athanasius the Great, *On the Incarnation* (Crestwood, NY: St. Vladimir's Seminary Press, 1996), 54.

63   St. Mark the Monk *On Baptism*. [AQ: Please add chapter and/or paragraph number.]

64   St. John Climacus, *The Ladder of Divine Ascent* (Boston, MA: Holy Transfiguration Monastery, 1991), 71.

65   Second Antiphon, Tone 4, Matins.

66   St. Basil the Great, *On the Holy Spirit*, trans. David Anderson (Crestwood, NY: St. Vladimir's Seminary Press), 43.

CHAPTER 7

67   Tertullian On Baptism 7.

68   Mother Maria (Rule), *Saints and Spirit-bearers: Models for Orthodox Women, Orthodox Women Speak* (Geneva: WCC Publications, 1999), 79.

69   St. Nicholas Cabasilas *Life in Christ* 4.3.

70   Archimandrite Sophrony Sakharov, *Saint Silouan the Athonite* (Essex, UK: Patriarchal Stavropegic Monastery of St. John the Baptist, 1991), 448–53.

71   Ibid., 326–27.

72   *The Ascetic of Love* (Thessaloniki, Gerece: Talanto, 2006) 208.

73   St. Augustine, *Confessions*, trans. R.S. Pine-Coffin (New York: Penguin, 1961), 21.

CHAPTER 8

74   St. John of Kronstadt, *My Life in Christ*, (Jordanville, NY: Holy Trinity Monastery, 1994) 407.
75   Elder Paisios of the Holy Mountain, *With Pain and Love for Contemporary Man* (Thessaloniki, Greece: Holy Monastery "Evangelist John the Theologian," 2007), 342.
76   St. Nicholas Cabasilas, *A Commentary on the Divine Liturgy*, trans. J.M. Hussey and P.A. McNulty (London: SPCK, 1960), 91.

CHAPTER 9

77   William Shakespeare, *Hamlet*, Act 2, Scene 2.
78   First Ode, Matins, Canon of the Akathist.
79   Archimandrite Sophrony Sakharov, *Saint Silouan the Athonite* (Essex, UK: Patriarchal Stavropegic Monastery of St. John the Baptist, 1991), 326.
80   Akathist Troparion, Feast of the Annunciation, Tone 3.
81   Archimadrite Sophrony Sakharov, *Saint Silouan the Athonite* (Essex, UK: Patriarchal Stravropegic Monastery of St. John the Baptist, 1991) 387.
82   Archimandrite Sophrony Sakharov, *We Shall See Him As He Is* (Essex, UK: Patriarchal Stavropegic Monastery of St. John the Baptist, 2008), 194.
83   Benedicta Ward, trans., *The Sayings of the Desert Fathers* (Kalamazoo, MI: Cistercian, 1975), 103.

About Paraclete Press

Who We Are

Paraclete Press is a publisher of books, recordings, and DVDs on Christian spirituality. Our publishing represents a full expression of Christian belief and practice—from Catholic to Evangelical, from Protestant to Orthodox.

We are the publishing arm of the Community of Jesus, an ecumenical monastic community in the Benedictine tradition. As such, we are uniquely positioned in the marketplace without connection to a large corporation and with informal relationships to many branches and denominations of faith.

What We Are Doing

BOOKS

Paraclete publishes books that show the richness and depth of what it means to be Christian. Although Benedictine spirituality is at the heart of all that we do, we publish books that reflect the Christian experience across many cultures, time periods, and houses of worship. We publish books that nourish the vibrant life of the church and its people—books about spiritual practice, formation, history, ideas, and customs.

We have several different series, including the best-selling Paraclete Essentials and Paraclete Giants series of classic texts in contemporary English; A Voice from the Monastery—men and women monastics writing about living a spiritual life today; award-winning literary faith fiction and poetry; and the Active Prayer Series that brings creativity and liveliness to any life of prayer.

RECORDINGS

From Gregorian chant to contemporary American choral works, our music recordings celebrate sacred choral music through the centuries. Paraclete distributes the recordings of the internationally acclaimed choir Gloriæ Dei Cantores, praised for their "rapt and fathomless spiritual intensity" by *American Record Guide*, and the Gloriæ Dei Cantores Schola, which specializes in the study and performance of Gregorian chant. Paraclete is also the exclusive North American distributor of the recordings of the Monastic Choir of St. Peter's Abbey in Solesmes, France, long considered to be a leading authority on Gregorian chant.

DVDs

Our DVDs offer spiritual help, healing, and biblical guidance for life issues: grief and loss, marriage, forgiveness, anger management, facing death, and spiritual formation.

Learn more about us at our website:
www.paracletepress.com, or call us toll-free at 1-800-451-5006.

Also in this series...

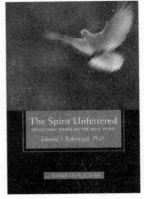

The Spirit Unfettered
Protestant Views on the Holy Spirit

by Edmund J. Rybarczyk

$15.99   Trade paperback
ISBN: 978-1-55725-654-6

This clear guide will help you understand what is distinctive about Protestant
perspectives on who the Holy Spirit is and what the Holy Spirit does
in our lives.

The introduction broadly compares Protestant views on the Holy
Spirit with Roman Catholic and Eastern Orthodox models. The
understandings of important theologians and figures in Protestant
tradition such as Luther, the Anabaptists, Wesley, Pinnock, and Barth
as well as living theologians such as Jurgen Moltmann, Wolfhart
Pannenberg, and Michael Welker are also explored.

*"We can be grateful to God that so many Christians in recent years have
experienced the power of the Holy Spirit in new ways. But the time is long past
for the whole Church to claim that renewing power, both theologically and
experientially. This fine book points us to the theological resources—drawn
from a variety of Christian traditions—to move ahead with that urgent task!"*

—Dr. Richard J. Mouw, President
Fuller Theological Seminary